THE PUBLIC SERVANT'S GUIDE
TO GOVERNMENT IN CANADA

Second Edition

THE PUBLIC SERVANT'S GUIDE TO GOVERNMENT IN CANADA

Second Edition

Alex Marland and Jared J. Wesley

UNIVERSITY OF TORONTO PRESS
Toronto Buffalo London

© University of Toronto Press 2025
Toronto Buffalo London
utppublishing.com
Printed in Canada

ISBN 978-1-4875-6086-7 (EPUB)
ISBN 978-1-4875-6084-3 (paper)   ISBN 978-1-4875-6085-0 (PDF)

Library and Archives Canada Cataloguing in Publication

Title: The public servant's guide to government in Canada / Alex Marland and Jared J. Wesley.
Names: Marland, Alex, 1973–, author | Wesley, Jared J., 1980–, author
Description: Second edition. | Includes bibliographical references and index.
Identifiers: Canadiana (print) 20250124467 | Canadiana (ebook) 20250124505 | ISBN 9781487560843 (paper) | ISBN 9781487560867 (EPUB) | ISBN 9781487560850 (PDF)
Subjects: LCSH: Civil service – Canada. | LCSH: Civil service – Canada – Handbooks, manuals, etc. | LCSH: Public administration – Canada. | LCSH: Public administration – Canada – Handbooks, manuals, etc. | LCSH: Civil service positions – Canada. | LCGFT: Handbooks and manuals.
Classification: LCC JL108 .M368 2025 | DDC 352.6/30971 – dc23

Cover design: John Beadle
Cover image: Yurkaimmortal/Vector Stock

We welcome comments and suggestions regarding any aspect of our publications – please feel free to contact us at news@utorontopress.com or visit us at utppublishing.com.

Every effort has been made to contact copyright holders; in the event of an error or omission, please notify the publisher.

We wish to acknowledge the land on which the University of Toronto Press operates. This land is the traditional territory of the Wendat, the Anishnaabeg, the Haudenosaunee, the Métis, and the Mississaugas of the Credit First Nation.

University of Toronto Press acknowledges the financial support of the Government of Canada and the Ontario Arts Council, an agency of the Government of Ontario, for its publishing activities.

CONTENTS

FIGURES, TABLES, AND BOXES

WHO SHOULD READ THIS BOOK

This book is intended for anyone who wants to better understand their place as a government employee in Canada, or who aspires to be one. Anyone who has not completed a post-secondary program in public administration will benefit from becoming acquainted with key theories and practices about government. Current public servants, particularly recent hires and those without experience in executive-level positions, will gain familiarity with concepts that will help them better recognize where they fit in the public service. Students and recent graduates who avail of experiential learning opportunities such as practicums, internships, or co-operative education programs will learn the basics and nuances of working in the public service and advancing their career.

We are committed to improving this book and animating its content. Readers are invited to contact us with revision suggestions, or to explore the possibility of us addressing groups of aspiring and current public servants.

ACKNOWLEDGEMENTS

Many reviewers provided feedback to improve the contents of this book, ranging from conceptual comments to practical advice. We appreciate the detailed input provided to the University of Toronto Press from two anonymous referees and from several practitioners who offered helpful suggestions, including Sean Dutton, Deborah G. Young, and Kimberly Armstrong. In addition, we collected tips and feedback from current and former public servants and political personnel as well as our students and instructors from across Canada. The authors also appreciate the input received from various public servants, political staffers, and students. We continue to welcome further suggestions from readers.

CHAPTER 1

DEFINING THE PUBLIC GOOD

Many public servants stand on the front lines of Canadian democracy. They deliver programs and services, engage Canadians on policy changes, perhaps offer advice to cabinet ministers, and might work in concert with political staff to refine and execute the government's agenda. Given these wide-ranging and influential roles, public servants need a firm grounding in the principles of politics and governance in Canada. They must understand how the public interest is determined and recognize their own role in achieving the public good. A refresher for some and a primer for others, this chapter summarizes these basic ground rules of Canadian democracy. We begin by defining who we mean by *public servants*.

What Is a Public Servant?

A public servant is an employee of the government. In a democracy, government – and thus public servants – should make life better for society and the general public. We focus on the *non-partisan* workers in the core public service, which in federal and provincial governments refers to politically neutral employees working in departments, Crown corporations, and agencies. They are alternatively known as civil servants and bureaucrats, but for consistency we refer to them mostly as public servants. This encompasses the permanent, salaried personnel in government and those on contracts, including short-term staff such as interns and co-operative education students. Comparative analysis across federal and provincial organizations reveals a series of

TABLE 1.1 Occupation Areas in the Canadian Public Service

FIELDS	ROLE EXAMPLES
Administrative Support	Clerical, correspondence, data processing
Corporate	Planning, finance, human resources
General Labour/Trades	Maintenance, construction, printing
General Services	Custodial, food services
Operations	Client services, program support, regulation, inspection
Policy	Research, analysis, design
Strategy	Intergovernmental relations, communications
Technical/Professional	Lawyers, social workers, scientists

common functional areas. These are illustrated in Table 1.1. Many of these fields exist in territorial, municipal, and Indigenous governments as well. The roles and responsibilities of these employees – the vast majority of whom were not required to have studied public administration or political science – are the focus of this guide.

Politicians and political staff are also featured in this book because they work closely with senior public servants and are the ones who guide public policy. In large governments, public servants who work on the front lines interacting with the public spend little time, if any, directly interacting with politically connected people in executive offices. Some go through their entire career without meeting a political decision-maker. Conversely, in small governments there is more interactivity between elected government officials and street-level bureaucrats.

Other people on the public payroll are not strictly considered public servants because government is not their primary employer. Public sector workers such as teachers, nurses, doctors, professors, military personnel, police and corrections officers, and others are subject to their own professional codes. They have their own separate training facilities, regulatory bodies, associations, and unions. What all of them have in common is that public sector workers are paid, at least in part, using public money. Moreover, they are all subject to decisions made by a relatively small number of executives with legitimate authority to steer and oversee the government. Those executives sit at the intersection between political jousting among politicians and the neutral, apolitical work of the public service. Conversely, a public servant's area of expertise can attract media attention, be deliberated in the legislature, be debated on social media and discussed in an election campaign – without public servants themselves being involved in the public discourse. They usually keep their own opinions about government to themselves, as these might or might not align with those of the politicians in charge. Upholding the crucial principle of professional neutrality can require navigating a delicate equilibrium between politics and public administration.

Democracy and the Public Good

Democratic government is messy and confusing. *Democracy* means that the authority of those who govern is derived from the people being governed. This includes the ability to define what is in the public interest when identifying, prioritizing, and addressing pressing challenges. Not all members of the public can be engaged in this process equally. In large societies like Canada, asking electors to vote in referendums on every matter of public policy would be impractical. That is why we elect representatives to make important decisions on our behalf. For their part, politicians must balance short-term pressures with longer-term implications, and the desire to be re-elected with the imperatives of doing what they interpret to be the right thing for the greater good. Internally, many grapple with their responsibilities to represent not only constituents in their electoral districts, but also the interests of their political party (where applicable) and their own personal convictions. Among themselves, elected officials are motivated by competing ideologies, pressures, and agendas.

In a democracy there is a constant struggle over who gets what, pitting individuals and groups against one another. Anyone engaged with Canadian politics and government should understand that criticism is inevitable. Not all members of the public can be satisfied all the time. Some vent online and some attend rallies to protest government decisions, while others go as far as to initiate legal action or even challenge the very legitimacy of the regime. People publicly complaining about politics and government is a hallmark of a free society. The extent to which government personnel are aware of, concerned about, and positioned to respond to those demands determines their effectiveness in the eyes of Canadians. Even then, many individuals will be dissatisfied for an assortment of reasons. Many others are not paying attention, which can constitute tacit approval.

A general election is a peaceful way to sort out political conflict. In federal, provincial, and territorial arenas, voters come together at polling stations to determine which politicians should represent them and ultimately form a *cabinet* to direct the government. In parliamentary systems, the politicians with the most power are the ones in cabinet. These individuals distribute resources to implement campaign promises, and are held to account by other elected members of the legislature. Election results are seldom straightforward indicators of the public good, however. Election campaigns barely touch on all of the many issues a government must deal with, and voting involves trade-offs. An elector might like only certain aspects of a party's election platform, for instance, yet vote for their candidate anyway. Some voters simply place their trust in a party label, leader, or local candidate to do what's best without considering the policy promises. On occasion, the most popular party in terms of votes does not get to form government. At other times, events conspire to derail a government's agenda and thrust new sets of decisions upon them that had not been incorporated into their election platform. As well, prime ministers and premiers can get forced out of office by their own party, which then identifies someone else to head up the government. In short, while they are fundamental to democracy, elections do not settle all debates over what constitutes the public interest or even who governs.

Instead, the competition of ideas persists post-election. We hear about some politicking, such as protests by organized interests and activists that attract news coverage. Much goes unnoticed, such as private meetings among politicians and the representatives of businesses, labour unions, and other organized interests. Members of cabinet and the legislature channel their constituents' concerns and have their own personal views and priorities. Politicians typically weigh all available information as they seek to advance a political agenda and shape the norms, practices, decisions, and rules of government. Collectively, those outcomes are known as *public policy*: what governments do or do not do.

There are several phases in public policy, discussed in greater detail in **Chapter 3**. Ideas attract public attention and are debated, developed, implemented, and evaluated. At each phase, public servants and political staff perform various interdependent functions. This process of *public administration* is not itself a democracy. It is not up to public servants to decide policy or to comment publicly on it; in a parliamentary system of government, that is the role of *ministers*. Instead, public servants must follow what is known as the *public service bargain*, discussed in **Chapter 2**. They should provide fearless advice to their political masters and, when a political choice is made, loyally implement that decision within the bounds of the law. Public servants must therefore prevent their personal views from interfering with their ability to dutifully follow a chain of command. A functional bureaucracy depends on an efficient organizational hierarchy of skilled, trustworthy, and loyal employees. This helps ensure that employees throughout the public service always act on behalf of ministers, who are members of the governing party that the electorate entrusted with the authority to make decisions. In no sense are public servants expected to serve as effective checks on the authority of elected governments. There are other institutions in place for that purpose.

> **Tip: Respect Ministerial Authority**
> Public servants must separate their own personal agendas from the government's agenda. Public servants do not have the right or legitimacy to determine what is in the public's interest, or to judge what makes for good public policy. Ministers do.

Power and the Constitution

Governments make a multitude of decisions that have an impact on Canadians' lives in very real ways. Public policies dictate how fast we can drive a vehicle or receive medical care, when we can leave the country or play loud music outside, where we can set up a business or walk our unleashed pets, who we can marry or hire, what we can put in our luggage or gardens, or how much we can donate to a political party or purchase at a pharmacy. The power to make these and other decisions needs to be divided, whether out of efficiency or a desire to avoid concentrating too much authority in the hands of too few. The nuances of power-sharing are not obvious, even to those who have spent a lifetime working in public administration.

Understanding how government works begins by recognizing that Canada, as we know it today, continues to evolve through a complex process of colonization. This happened in two fundamental ways: specific governing structures imposed by the French and British imperial states to manage territory and resources; and the social, cultural, religious, and economic structures introduced and extended by the various settler populations. There was almost no consultation with *Indigenous Peoples* about any of this. The various treaties and proclamations of the eighteenth century offer examples of Indigenous Peoples being excluded from negotiations or being forced to confront settlers who refused to recognize what was agreed in those documents. The establishment of the "Indian Department" by the British government in 1755 was an important indicator of what lay ahead, including its successor, the Department of Indian Affairs and Northern Development. The oppression and attempted assimilation of Indigenous Peoples that this activity enabled was calculated, and Section 91 of the *Constitution Act, 1867*, for example, outlines the legislative authority of the Parliament of Canada and assigns jurisdiction over "Indians and lands reserved for Indians." Other parts of the constitution protect Aboriginal and treaty rights. Negotiations over jurisdiction have led to land claim settlements and increasing recognition of systems of Indigenous self-governance within the boundaries of the Canadian constitution and federation.[1]

Many observers view these and other legal principles as subjugating Indigenous Peoples to the authority of the federal government. This was borne out in the government funding church-run residential schools and the forced relocation of thousands of *First Nations, Inuit,* and *Métis* children as a means of assimilating Indigenous Peoples into Canadian society. The *Truth and Reconciliation Commission*'s (TRC) 2015 report revealed the intergenerational impact of the schools. To varying degrees, public servants are involved in addressing these injustices in line with political and legal decisions. Governments across Canada have committed to addressing the TRC's calls to action, but

1 Papillon, "Adapting Federalism."

progress has been "glacial," including call number 57, which recommends the establishment of mandatory Indigenous awareness training for public servants.[2] Public servants should seek out these learning opportunities, regardless of whether they are compulsory parts of their workplace training.

> **Tip: Explore Indigenous Histories and Perspectives**
> The University of Alberta runs an award-winning, free, online course that teaches participants about the unique perspectives of Indigenous Peoples. Search "Indigenous Canada course" to start the twelve-week program.

All told, across the country hundreds of individual First Nations, Inuit, and Métis nations exist. These Indigenous communities have various modes of representation, some self-determined (like systems led by hereditary chiefs), others imposed by the Canadian state (like the band system organized under the *Indian Act*). Larger Indigenous governments have developed complex bureaucracies that resemble those found in mid-size municipalities. Likewise, Indigenous Peoples interact with the Canadian state in various ways. There are national Indigenous organizations that meet routinely with the federal minister of Indigenous affairs, for instance, and regional Indigenous governments representing people in different treaty areas and provinces. All public servants bear a responsibility to be aware of these relationships.

This awareness includes understanding that the constitution lays out the foundations of the Canadian state. Ultimately, political power in Canada is derived from the constitution – a body of written documents, unwritten conventions, and key court rulings that organize government and society.[3] Primary among these rules, the *Constitution Act*s outline how government authority is distributed within and among governments, while since 1982 the *Canadian Charter of Rights and Freedoms* has enshrined protections for citizens against government overreach.

Specifically, Canada is a constitutional monarchy built on the institutions of parliamentary democracy and *federalism*. The King of the

---

2 Jewell and Mosby, *Calls to Action Accountability.*
3 Macfarlane, "The Place of Constitutional Conventions."

United Kingdom and the King of Canada are separate and distinct offices, although they are occupied by the same person. The monarch is represented in Canada by the *governor general*, an Ottawa-based official who takes advice from the prime minister when appointing a *lieutenant governor* to represent the Crown in each provincial capital. Commissioners fulfill a similar role in the territories. These individuals' responsibilities as the *Crown* largely encompass ceremonial functions, such as reading speeches and bestowing awards. More substantively, they give assent to bills by signing them into law and have the power to appoint and dismiss governments. Almost all of the Crown's powers are executed based on advice from governments that hold the confidence of their respective legislatures. The monarch's representative plays little role in determining what is in the public interest and, in fact, normally avoids getting involved in any activity that could be interpreted as political or partisan. Nonetheless, in specific instances, the Crown is empowered to refuse requests from the head of government to restart or dissolve a parliamentary assembly and, in extreme cases, can opt to dismiss a government that is abusing power.

The Canadian constitution divides power in several ways, preventing it from being concentrated in the hands of a few. The authority to define the public interest is distributed along geographic lines, for instance. Canada is a *federation*, meaning that legislative power is divided between a national (federal) government and ten provincial governments. Section 91 of the *Constitution Act, 1867*, assigns authority to the Government of Canada for areas including the military, postal service, immigration, and many economic instruments such as currency, banking, and trade. Section 92 provides provincial governments with authority over lands, hospitals, municipalities, education, non-renewable resources, and many forms of licensing. The three territories are within the constitutional jurisdiction of the federal government. Their powers are largely delegated by Parliament, subject to any devolution agreements. As mentioned, much of this book is about how the federal and provincial governments work.

Municipalities are of growing importance in Canada and yet they have a minor status in constitutional order. The *Constitution Act, 1867* stipulates that provincial legislatures have exclusive authority to make laws about municipalities. Forms of local government range from cities, towns, and villages, to counties, townships, and special-purpose bodies.

Each has its own unique governance structure, internal dynamics, and way of dealing with other levels of government. Local politics and elections are likewise different from place to place. A notable difference is the near absence of political parties in municipal politics, except in some large cities. Decision-making processes depend largely on the size of the community and whether representatives are elected to represent geographic constituencies (e.g., wards) or on an at-large basis (e.g., an entire city or town). Power may be concentrated at the top of the organization – within the office of the mayor or an executive committee – or distributed across elected councillors or within committees. In many municipalities, the bureaucracy is known as "administration." Composed of full-time, permanent employees, a municipal administration can wield considerable policy-making authority, reporting periodically to council. Employees working for a municipal government are far more likely to engage with municipal politicians than their federal or provincial counterparts are likely to interact with ministers. As a result, the role of bureaucrats in local government resembles that of their federal/provincial/territorial colleagues in some ways and differs in others.

Turning back to how the federal and provincial governments are organized, the power to determine the public good is divided among three branches: the executive, which is responsible for establishing priorities and developing policy; the legislature, tasked with overseeing the executive by passing, amending, and repealing laws, including budget proposals; and the judiciary, which applies and interprets those laws. Of note, public servants are part of the executive branch, which some observers consider the most powerful of the three.

The politicians at the top of the executive branch normally simultaneously hold seats in the elected legislature. The party that wins the most seats in a general election usually forms government, with its leader becoming the *first minister*. Known as the *prime minister* or *premier*, this individual typically forms a cabinet by choosing elected members of the governing party to serve as *ministers*. It is the Crown's representative who formally appoints them. While contributing to overall government decisions, each minister provides political leadership for a department and series of agencies that deal with a particular area of public policy, like health care or natural resources. First ministers prize personal and party loyalty when selecting members to cabinet, as well as other imperatives like achieving regional representation and demographic balance.

The first minister and cabinet ministers are the key decision-makers in the executive branch, and they are constrained by a system known as *responsible government*.[4] Put simply, politicians in a parliamentary government must maintain the support of most members of the legislature if they want to continue making major policy decisions. Securing the votes of a majority of legislators on key pieces of proposed legislation and the budget demonstrates that the government holds the confidence of the legislature. Those parliamentarians are, in turn, held to account by voters through regular elections. This means that if enough people raise enough concern among enough of their elected representatives, a prime minister, premier, and their ministers must respond upon pain of removal. This is the way that responsible government works in theory. In practice, the concentration of power in executive offices and strict party discipline imposed upon legislators reduce the constraints placed on senior government officials.

Cabinet is the source of most important political decisions, which are often translated as minutes in council for the public service to carry out. To manage the volume and importance of business, each government usually maintains several cabinet committees. Small groups of ministers meet to study an issue and make recommendations to the full cabinet. Regardless of their positions in private, all ministers must publicly support cabinet decisions. This principle of cabinet solidarity ensures a measure of collective responsibility. It also prevents ministers from disowning unpopular decisions and creating confusion over what constitutes authoritative government policy. As a result, in public a minister will effuse support for government policy, regardless of whether they personally agree with it.

A bit of a grey area is the existence of *parliamentary secretaries*, known as associate ministers or ministerial assistants in some jurisdictions. They do not normally have cabinet status. The role is best seen as a training ground for elected representatives who hope to one day be appointed to cabinet. A parliamentary secretary rarely, if ever, attends cabinet meetings or participates in decision-making. Rather, they attend to matters delegated by the minister they are assigned to assist.

....

4 Birch, *Representative and Responsible Government*.

Complexity and Coordination

If democracy is messy, then it follows that government needs to be effectively run and organized. Cabinets face considerable challenges in coordinating information and decision-making across dozens of ministries. Indeed, without the capacity to synchronize policy, governments would fall victim to several collective-action problems. Resources would be spent inefficiently, ministers might work competitively or at cross-purposes, and directives could be miscommunicated as they make their way from the first minister to the minister to the bureaucracy. These challenges persist even with the advent of *central agencies* to coordinate policy-making, but they would be even more acute without them.

At the federal level, information about the whole of government flows through two main central bodies: the Prime Minister's Office (PMO), which handles partisan considerations that help the governing party get re-elected, and the *Privy Council Office* (PCO), which is responsible for non-partisan support on public policy matters. So much power is concentrated in the PMO that their senior staff exercise decision-making authority comparable to (or even exceeding) some ministers. The chief of staff heads the PMO and is understood to speak for the prime minister when dealing with members of cabinet, caucus, the senior public service, other governments' officials, and so on. The PMO includes a variety of other senior advisors, communications professionals, planners, regional officers, issues managers, executive assistants, and staff dedicated to supporting the prime minister and coordinating the work across ministries. The chief of staff appoints ministerial chiefs of staff, sometimes against the wishes of the minister. A minister's office is a miniature version of the PMO, with staff coordinating the minister's affairs, implementing directives from the prime minister's staff, and feeding intelligence and advice back into their central office. The political staff who work in the PMO and ministers' offices are affiliated with the governing party and often worked on the election campaign that brought it to power.

Working in tandem with the PMO, the PCO provides non-partisan support at the highest level of the federal government. Public servants who work in the PCO deliver briefings to the prime minister and cabinet, coordinate cabinet operations, develop intergovernmental strategy, conduct cross-sector policy analysis, prepare speeches, and so forth. The PCO is led by the most senior public servant, the *clerk*. In addition to serving as one of the prime minister's lead policy advisors and as secretary to cabinet, the clerk heads the non-partisan public service including the *deputy ministers* (DMs) assigned as the head of each ministry. Collectively, these senior personnel and their staff mobilize the public service to deliver the government's agenda, ensure policy coordination across government, and participate in the implementation of cabinet decisions, document control, and executive-level briefings. Similar central agencies support premiers at the provincial/territorial level, where the *Premier's Office* wields substantial political control over ministers and the Executive Council Office (ECO) or equivalent fulfills many of the same functions as the PCO.

> **Tip: Seek Central Agency Experience**
> Working within a central agency or a policy coordination unit within a ministry can provide a broader perspective on policy development and public administration, and impart experience in strategy, issues management, agility, and diplomacy. In some governments, employment at the upper echelon of government is a pathway to promotion to senior management roles within line departments.

Together, the prime minister or premier, the cabinet, the chief of staff, and the clerk sit atop each government's organizational pyramid. The political staff and senior public servants working in the PCO/ECO and other central agencies (including the Department of Finance and the Treasury Board Secretariat) are commonly known as the *centre of government*. Ministers, deputy ministers, and departmental public servants are expected to follow requests from the centre and supply information to the central agencies (Figure 1.1). The roles of the Finance and Treasury Board are especially important when matters of government spending or revenues are at stake. We discuss their role in the budget cycle as part of **Chapter 3**. As well, deputy ministers maintain connections with their counterparts in other ministries. This is illustrated in Figure 1.2. The PMO or Premier's Office maintains

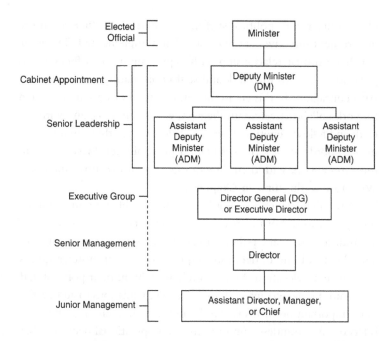

FIGURE 1.1 Senior Hierarchy in a Government Department

Note: Members of cabinet are ordinarily elected officials. In rare cases when they do not hold a seat in the legislature, common practice dictates that they do so at the earliest opportunity, such as by winning a by-election. Deputy ministers are senior public servants appointed through an Order in Council, which is normally requested by the first minister and not subject to cabinet discussion.

Source: Adapted from various organization charts in provincial and federal government ministries.

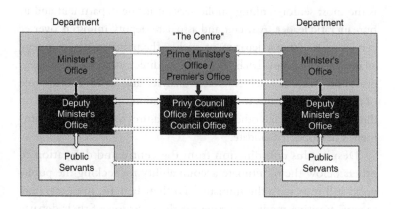

FIGURE 1.2 The Power Structure in Canadian Governments

close contact with political staff in each minister's office to ensure government directives are understood and implemented. The PCO/ECO has a similar relationship with deputy ministers' offices across government, with the clerk and staff coordinating work with the DM's colleagues. In this environment, deputy ministers are expected to work collaboratively with their respective ministers, and with the clerk and fellow deputies. They are leaders within their own departments, coordinating various assistant deputy ministers (ADMs) who, in turn, must work with their directors general or executive directors. We return to this topic in **Chapter 4**.

Naturally, cabinet does not have time to deliberate on all public policy decisions. For this reason, governments pass laws empowering ministers to make policy choices in their respective portfolios. The sheer volume of decisions required of each minister requires even further delegation. Ministers rely heavily on their political staff and senior public servants to provide recommendations to address the most important problems facing the ministry. In addition, a minister is faced with countless administrative and operational decisions that need to be made every day, such as the awarding of grants and small contracts, nominating people to serve on boards, or reporting to cabinet committees. These are normally channelled to heads of government agencies or the deputy minister through legislation, mandate letters, and performance agreements. Appointed by the first minister, overseen by the clerk, and serving at the pleasure of the cabinet, the DM is the most senior-ranking public servant in the department and its bureaucratic leader. Assistant and associate deputy ministers oversee certain areas within a department, such as the policy group, corporate affairs, or operations. Each area employs directors to whom managers report, who themselves oversee analysts, and so on. It is the role of these public servants to provide information up the line, to act on directives, and to take other necessary measures to fulfill the government's democratic mandate.

Despite this coordination from the centre and delegation to others below them, ultimate accountability for seeking the public good still rests with the minister. To their benefit, ministers may receive positive media coverage for the successes of their department. Conversely, the minister is the departmental spokesperson

Tip: Stay in Your Lane

Most interactions among political staff and public servants occur among senior officials, particularly in larger governments. If you are a public servant and find yourself working with political staff, remember that – while your objectives may align in most cases – your mandates are distinct. As a non-partisan public servant, it is your role to support the government in fulfilling its agenda. Good policy and top-notch programs and services will improve the government's standing with voters, but it is not your job to advocate a partisan agenda or help politicians get re-elected. That responsibility falls to political staff.

when there is a controversial decision or blunder. If mistakes are made, the minister is accountable to the prime minister (or premier) and the legislature through the concept of ministerial responsibility, discussed in **Chapter 4**.

In these ways, accountability in the parliamentary system becomes complex. If unelected partisans in the PMO are deeply embedded in influencing policy, who is to hold the real decision-makers to account? Under responsible government, the legislature empowers the government to enact its agenda. Put another way, cabinet must demonstrate it has the confidence of the legislature in order to pursue major policy initiatives or engage in government spending. The elected assembly is a forum to debate bills introduced by ministers and private members. Parliamentarians can register their disapproval by voting down major policy, such as the annual budget. Alternatively, a motion of non-confidence in the government can be introduced so that they can register a lack of support for the government continuing. If a major government initiative is defeated or a non-confidence motion passes, the governor general or lieutenant governor typically dissolves the legislature, triggering a general election. This causes new people to be elected, some of whom will be appointed to form a new cabinet, while others retire or are not re-elected. An election can also lead to a different political party and its leader assuming control of the government.

In other words, a majority of the people's elected representatives must approve of what the cabinet is doing. On the surface, this approval requirement ought to place a check on cabinet's authority. The executive and legislative branches are effectively fused, however, because most if not all members of the executive are concurrently a sitting member of the legislature and part of the governing party's caucus. This fusion of powers distinguishes parliamentary democracies like Canada from other types of government, as in the United States, where there is a separation of powers between the executive and legislative branches.

In Westminster parliamentary systems like Canada, many members of the legislature who are affiliated with the governing party do not have a formal role in the executive and are therefore not part of the government. Along with their counterparts from other parties, they are known as backbenchers because, as a sign of their lesser role, their chairs literally fill out the back spots in a legislative chamber. The first minister wields considerable control over these government backbenchers through party discipline, reducing the likelihood that any would speak out against the government outside of closed caucus meetings, let alone vote against it. Furthermore, they communicate information about government decisions and actions to their constituents, often with a celebratory tone. Thus, while backbenchers on the government side of the House are not part of the government, they can appear as though they are.[5]

The executive enjoys greater autonomy from the legislative branch when more than half the members of the legislature sit on the government benches. These *majority government* scenarios allow the governing party to implement an agenda with little concern for opposition parties' opinions. During these periods, public servants are more likely to see long term policy proposals advance. Conversely, in a *minority government* situation, the risk of a snap election creates instability and there is greater emphasis on immediate policy solutions and spending. Controlling fewer than half the seats makes governing more difficult because the party in power needs to pay more attention to opposition opinion. Even then, members of other political parties have limited power over government decision-making, however.

....
5 Marland, Wesley, and Lalancette, *No "I" in Team.*

The party with the second-highest number of seats usually assumes the mantle of Official Opposition. The leader of the opposition designates a shadow cabinet, whereby some opposition members of the legislature formally act as public critics for given ministers. In the legislature, opposition parties attempt to hold the government to account through question period and parliamentary committees. They may use procedural delay to frustrate the ability of the governing party to pass bills in a timely manner. Outside the legislature, the leader of the Official Opposition commands media attention, and to a lesser extent so do the leaders of any other parties. Their perspectives often disrupt government plans but, in the absence of toppling the government on a matter of confidence, opposition parties are seldom able to thwart them entirely. Instead, the opposition upholds the traditions of liberal democracy, providing alternative voices and plans that compete for favour among voters at elections. A well-run opposition party presents itself as a government-in-waiting.

In many ways, the judicial branch plays a more effective check on executive power than the legislature. Whether at the local, provincial, or national level, the decisions and actions of all legislative bodies and governments are subject to legal interpretation. In Canada, the rule of law ensures nobody is above reproach or accountability, including those holding high office. The judiciary serves as the guardian of this principle, ensuring that all laws passed by a legislature are compliant with the constitution, including the *Charter of Rights and Freedoms*. Activists, interest groups, businesses, and concerned citizens sometimes initiate court challenges to test the constitutionality of legislation. Judges may find that a law does not adequately address a situation. They might make legal interpretations that differ with public opinion, create policy where one does not exist, or refer an issue to the legislature to ensure a law is constitutional. In this way, the rule of law rises above partisan politics, as the judicial branch weighs legal arguments away from political theatre.

The Supreme Court of Canada is the final court of appeal and sets out the ultimate interpretation of the constitution. Supreme Court justices are appointed by the governor general on the advice of the prime minister. Similar processes occur at the provincial level for lower court judges. Idealistically, this results in non-partisan appointments when an independent appointments commission or similar process is in place; in reality, appointees to the bench hold similar values as the governing party. Moreover, while a court may be an arbiter, its decisions are by no means neutral in their effects on public policy. Historically, the Supreme Court has made many monumental decisions, in effect determining what constitutes the public interest and how best to secure it. This includes hot-button issues like prostitution and medical assistance in dying. It also includes overturning government decisions on matters like universal health care and settling jurisdictional disputes among governments, such as inter-provincial trade.

The power to define the public good is both divided and contested in Canada. While at the heart of our democracy, elections are imperfect mechanisms for setting the public policy agenda. Political parties may campaign on a set of promises, but many voters seldom read platforms and a governing party routinely confronts problems in office that require it to go off script. After an election, the capacity of ministers to push back on the power of central agencies or the ability of parliamentarians to hold those ministers to account is weaker than the responsible government model demands. So once governments are formed, they rely on public servants to provide them with the expertise needed to help guide them in their pursuit of the common interest.

Chapter Takeaways

This chapter establishes that public servants play an important, but highly structured, role in Canadian democracy. It focused on the executive-level structure of federal and provincial governments.

- Public servants carry out their work in a non-partisan manner. Senior public servants work in tandem with the first minister and/or cabinet minister(s) as well as political staff to help implement the government's agenda.
- Public servants serve Canadian society and the public. They are directly accountable to their superiors, and ultimately to their ministers.
- Public servants do not make public policy decisions. They provide advice to elected officials and carry out the directives they receive from cabinet.

- Public servants are part of a complex system of government. To perform effectively and avoid overstepping their authority, they must understand how their responsibilities intersect with elected, appointed, and partisan officials from all three branches (executive, legislative, judicial).

- From the frontlines to the deputy minister's office, public servants at all levels must actively engage in reconciliation, the first step of which is understanding the histories and perspectives of Indigenous Peoples in Canada.

CHAPTER 2

THE PUBLIC SERVICE BARGAIN

Prime ministers, premiers, and their ministers need specialized advice from non-partisan public servants to help them make policy decisions. The cabinet must be able to rely upon a highly qualified workforce that can present them with options and outline the potential implications of those choices, including ones that would spark public outrage. To have the courage to provide politicians with such frank advice, public servants must have job security, along with protections to prevent them from being drawn into political debate. This at the heart of what is known as the *public service bargain*, and it informs the way governments structure themselves in democracies like Canada.

Defining the Bargain

The roots of the public service bargain can be traced to the writings of German sociologist Max Weber in the nineteenth century. He maintained that it is imperative that governments operate in a highly efficient manner. The characteristics of a *Weberian bureaucracy* are recognizable in Canada today.[1] It holds that there must be an organizational hierarchy with employees following a chain of command. There must be formal rules, and employees must operate within those boundaries. Public servants must be specialists who can apply their expertise to a variety of situations. Internal governance must be neutral to ensure that staff

....

1 For more information on Weber's influence on public administration in Canada, see Sutherland and Doern, *Bureaucracy in Canada*.

in similar situations are treated in a reasonably identical manner, without favouritism. Thus, there must be standardized hiring and firing, which encourages the most meritorious to apply for positions and brings job security for those fulfilling their roles. Ideally this should produce a functional workplace that values specialized skill sets, ensures that directives are followed, and maintains norms and processes.

In the years that followed, public administration scholars built on Weber's view of a stand-alone bureaucracy. In the late nineteenth century, the permanency and accountability of the civil service was emphasized in the United States, as was the idea that public servants must be accountable to the politicians who are in turn held to account by the electorate.[2] Thinkers wrestled with the division of labour in government, concluding that elected officials and partisan staff ought to set the agenda for public servants to implement irrespective of their personal political views.

This separation of administration from politics broadened into what became known as the public service bargain. In the 1970s, scholars concluded that public servants must do the bidding of their political masters while upholding their legal obligations and public administration standards.[3] In return, ministers are the public face of the government, and are held accountable to the electorate that they serve. Ministers communicate and promote what they believe to be politically important. They publicly explain policies, receive credit for good news, and bear the brunt of blame when there are problems. Opinions that public servants should toil in obscurity support the underlying principles advanced by Weber.

This public service bargain allows government employees to work away from the media spotlight with a common understanding of the ground rules. Public servants benefit from job security compared with the relative precariousness of partisan jobs and employment in other sectors. They enjoy competitive compensation, including salary and pensions. Their employer engages in merit-based hiring and promotion practices that reward loyal, politically neutral service to the government of the day. Public servants should therefore avoid blatant political

....
2 Wilson, "The Study of Administration."
3 Schaffer, *The Administrative Factor.*

TABLE 2.1 The Public Service Bargain

ACTION	POLITICIANS IN CABINET	NON-PARTISAN PUBLIC SERVANTS
Provide:	Merit-based hiring and promotions Public accountability for decisions	Fearless advice Loyal implementation
Receive:	Evidence-informed advice Agenda execution	Competitive pay, benefits, job security Anonymity

interference in personnel decisions or distribution of government resources. These conventional trade-offs are captured in Table 2.1.

In the twenty-first century, this age-old approach to public administration is under threat.[4] Some critics question whether the bargain still exists.[5] Constitutional protections of democratic rights combined with the ability to communicate via social media are putting pressure on traditional views of a quiet, anonymous public service. Should public servants be allowed to say what they like on social media during their personal time on their private accounts? Or, as a condition of employment, should they be expected to always embody political neutrality? Should their professional advice be subject to freedom-of-information requests? Or should their recommendations to ministers be shielded from public view? Where you stand might depend on where you sit.

Compared to their colleagues in line departments, public servants who work in central agencies can experience a different set of expectations with respect to extracurricular political commentary and volunteering. It is still beyond the pale to expect these high-ranking public servants to get actively involved with the governing party in their spare time. Yet the scope of their work across government exposes them to more information and a greater perceived level of influence. This limits what they can say or do publicly. Public servants must be cautious about attracting attention as either supporting or undermining the governing party's chances at re-election, especially on matters that they work on directly.

....

4 Cole, "Public Service Bargains."

5 Savoie, *Breaking the Bargain.*

The public service bargain does not apply to all government employees. Deputy ministers, for example, do not have job security – they can be immediately dismissed. Some public servants work in what are known as "exempted" roles, like human resources or finance, placing them in a much closer relationship with public administration and the government as an employer. Staff in arm's-length agencies, boards, and commissions are not subject to the same deal, inasmuch as they work outside the confines of the public service. Instead, these public servants have separate contracts and codes of conduct that govern their relationship to their chief executive, who has a more formal accountability relationship with the minister than a deputy minister does.

The public service's bargain with elected officials also distinguishes public servants from their partisan counterparts. These members of the *political staff* often bring experience from the campaign trail and/or the private sector where bureaucratic norms are constantly challenged if not ignored. They have hardbound loyalties to one another. They have been on the front lines of interacting with Canadians and calls for change, and they have bonded over the high-stakes nature of elections. They do not have job protection the way that public servants do.

Ministers generally surround themselves with political staff who are astute. Politicos' desire to change the world often brings freshness, different perspectives, and originality. They can be a healthy counterbalance to the slow, cautious pace of government. Be careful, though: some political staff are unaware of the boundaries between politics, policy, and the public service bargain. Their expectations can be demanding and uninformed, perhaps even contrary to professional codes of values for public servants. Navigating the two different worlds is among the foremost challenges of political personnel seeking to advance a partisan agenda – and likewise for public servants who want a successful career.

This is where politics and public administration collide – part of what makes democracy messy. Even though they are all on the public payroll, public servants hired through the merit principle work in a different organizational environment than do ministers and political staff, who are political appointments. The public service has its own organizational culture. Public servants are anonymous, non-partisan, cautious, and follow lengthy consultation processes; political personnel are public figures to varying degrees, are hyper-partisan, are risk-takers, and prioritize immediacy. They are less focused on following rules to the letter or might not be aware of them, and yet their actions are subject to media and opposition scrutiny, as well as the whims of the PMO or Premier's Office. One group is relatively permanent, allowing them to engage in measured thinking and longer-term planning and implementation, while the other group is impermanent, impatient, and driven to win the next election campaign. These characteristics inform some of the core dynamics within government.

Threats to the Bargain

Concerns about the sanctity of the public service bargain have been voiced since the idea was first proposed.[6] Some worry about the politicization of the bureaucracy through the infusion of partisanship and a diminishing regard among some politicians and political staff for public service expertise. The appearance of senior public servants at parliamentary committee hearings, the surfacing on social media of internal email exchanges among public servants, and the public firing of bureaucrats for the failures of government have lifted the veil of anonymity that is integral to the bargain. Staff in the PMO and Premier's Office justify these breaches by distinguishing between ministers' "responsibility" to the legislature for the conduct of matters under their purview versus the "answerability" of public servants to account for decisions that were made (**Chapter 4**).

Governments of all partisan stripes have attempted to chip away at the public service bargain from a fiscal perspective. Beginning in the 1980s, the neoliberalism movement pushed for a reduction in the size of government and the compensation enjoyed by public servants as a means of cutting budget deficits and debt, as well as an increase in the role of the private sector in society and the economy. At different places and different times, this political agenda has sparked conflict between governments and public sector unions representing civil servants as well as teachers, nurses, and other public sector professionals.

Public servants across Canada are protected by *collective agreements* that guarantee certain labour standards, salary rates, leaves, seniority,

---

6 Hood and Dixon, *A Government That Worked Better and Cost Less?*

merit-based promotions, pensions, supplemental health benefits, remote work options, and other benefits. In the event of substandard performance, standardized disciplinary processes must be followed. Most governments extend a similar suite of benefits to non-unionized employees in management, directorship, and executive positions who often receive higher levels of compensation but lack the job protections of a unionized position. Periodically, unions must engage in *collective bargaining* with governments to extend or renegotiate these terms. Most collective agreements last less than four years, in theory allowing voters to weigh in on new deals in the subsequent election. In a unionized workplace, the merit principle can result in seniority being the deciding factor where promotion, redeployment, or layoffs are concerned.

From time to time, collective bargaining breaks down and collective agreements expire. Public servants who are unsatisfied with the status quo or the terms of a proposed settlement may opt to strike, bringing public attention to their plight. On the flip side, governments may lock out public servants, preventing them from working and receiving pay and benefits until a deal can be reached. Some public sector workers, such as nurses, have been deemed "essential workers" who must report to work even in the event of job action. In certain cases, governments have attempted to legislate public sector workers back to work, removing their right to strike altogether. Despite occasionally freezing salaries and hiring, governments have largely maintained their commitment to keeping public service salaries and benefits competitive with the private sector. In most jurisdictions, the size and compensation of the public service grow alongside the population and economy, and most public servants enjoy defined benefit pension plans that have disappeared from other parts of the workforce. New battlelines inevitably arise between governments and public sector unions, such as the ability to work from home.

Others see warning signs in the increased corporatization of the public service, which has shifted notions of accountability away from the principles of responsible government and toward client management and performance measurement.[7] The corporate-style delivery of public services represents what has become known as *New Public*

7 Honeghem and Van Dorpe, "Performance Management Systems."

Management (NPM).[8] The NPM trend was spurred by a quest in the 1980s for efficiencies and a private sector approach to organizing government. It involves privatization and automation of public services, the outsourcing of advice to paid consultants, businesslike internal management, and an emphasis on transparency and results. This includes a more customer-focused approach driven by managers empowered to find efficiencies, such as the use of e-government.

Proponents of NPM see value in separating strategic and operational policy-making, providing public servants with the authority to resolve situations as they arise. They also paint the reforms as being more open and democratic, particularly when it comes to results reporting and the expansion of freedom-of-information requests. Critics have raised concerns over conflating democracy with capitalism, treating the public as clients or stakeholders, and ignoring the value of public sector contributions beyond what can be measured by standard return on investment metrics. As well, in many governments the increased use of private consulting firms to develop policy has not coincided with a shrinking of the public service.

The New Public Management philosophy led to a Canadian twist, one that is more sinister. In the early 2000s, a Dalhousie University professor observed the politicization of public administration in Westminster systems like Canada and grouped his observations as a *New Political Governance* (NPG) model.[9] NPG reflects the implications of an evolving media environment, public expectations of transparency, performance auditing, intensifying political competition, and a polarized electorate. The public service is being politicized by these environmental pressures and the resulting strategic manoeuvres by partisans in government. NPG submits that governance is fusing with campaigning; that political staff are displacing senior public servants as trusted advisors; that public servants are expected to personally support the government's agenda; and that partisanship is therefore generally displacing impartiality. In short, political actors are infusing governments with their partisan agenda in ways that mimic the

8 Aucoin, *The New Public Management.*
9 Aucoin, "New Political Governance in Westminster Systems."

cut and thrust of party politics, in direct contravention of the public service bargain.

Those who study Canadian government exhibit less concern than their British counterparts do about the waning influence of public servants compared to political advisors and consultants. Nevertheless, Canadian political parties leverage all available public resources to promote a political agenda and support their re-election. This is known as *permanent campaigning*. It reflects a philosophy that the next election is just around the corner and shows a competitive drive to win every public battle. The language of government is infused with political rhetoric and spin, and transparency is shirked to avoid revealing controversial information. Government announcements are celebrated and timed for maximum advantage, and ministerial communications are thematically coordinated with the centre. Political strategists encourage the government to focus on subsets of the electorate to whom they promote targeted messages, as opposed to pursuing the greater good for the greatest number. These phenomena provide additional support for the existence of New Political Governance.

An additional threat to the public service bargain is that the role of senior public servants has drifted from being politically neutral, expert, and anonymous advisors to ministers. As government generally becomes more transparent – through proactive posting of information online, freedom-of-information requests, and public appearances by deputy ministers at parliamentary committee hearings, for instance – bureaucrats' ability to deliver frank, even controversial, advice is compromised by the possibility that their comments will end up in the public domain. At the same time, policy-making is an increasingly inter-sectoral affair that crosses multiple departments or spans the whole of government. This limits the capacity and need for deputy ministers to be intimately connected with the work of their respective departments. Deputies are chief executives, reflecting the businesslike spirit of New Public Management. As high-level managers, they tend to be policy generalists who are more adept at manoeuvring among their counterparts and key external stakeholders than at delivering in-depth advice on specific areas of policy.

Tip: Be Aware of Your Deputy Minister's Priorities

Most deputy ministers sign performance agreements with their clerk, outlining key policy, service, and corporate objectives for the year ahead. Knowing what your DM is accountable for doing can help you shape your own priorities. Some executives openly share their performance agreements with the staff who directly report to them.

The Public Servant's Mantra

So, if the public service bargain is under threat, what is a public servant to do? Public servants are well-advised to follow two prominent guideposts:

1. offer fearless advice to your superiors, and
2. loyally implement your superiors' lawful directives.

The origins of the Canadian public servant's mantra to offer "fearless advice and loyal implementation" are unclear. Alex Himelfarb, former federal clerk, used the expression in a 2002 speech. He urged public servants to focus on core values of "integrity and excellence in everything we do; respect for people, citizens, employees, colleagues, elected officials; embracing diversity as a source of strength; linguistic duality; and adaptability."[10] Himelfarb highlighted the skill sets of public servants as "rigorous policy analysis, creative policy options, innovative service delivery, effective resource management always focused on value for money, fearless advice, loyal implementation." Whatever the origins, the expression captures a way of thinking that pervades many areas of public administration in Canada. It requires a bit of context.

The idea of offering fearless advice is sometimes conflated with speaking truth to power. This romanticizes public servants as righteous purveyors of truth, and frames politicians as dishonest and manipulative. In reality, public servants offer information and

....
10 Himelfarb, "The Intermestic Challenge."

recommendations. Advice is tainted by their own biases based on their training, a risk-adverse culture, and as members of society. Moreover, the information public servants convey is only one part of the minister's decision-making process. There are many other considerations, including political ones we discuss in **Chapter 3**. This is why many refer to policy-making as being evidence-*informed* as opposed to evidence-*based*. Although evidence is often limited and provides a narrow view, it tends to be portrayed as more virtuous than political decisions driven by ideology, principles, or values. As noted, democracy is messy.

But the overall premise upholds the Weberian tradition. A public servant develops expertise and has job security for the purposes of conveying the best available information to those in higher positions. This manifests itself in comprehensive suites of options backed by detailed assessments of the implications of each choice. Informed opinions should be shared with honesty and without pandering to what politicians might want to hear. Ministers and high-ranking public servants do not generally have sufficient time, knowledge, skills, and/or authority to independently identify problems worth solving or solutions worth pursuing. They rely on rank-and-file analysts and managers to be creative and bold when identifying potential courses of action. The vitality and responsiveness of modern government depends upon public servants being detailed and forthcoming in terms of the potential risks and rewards involved.

Not everyone follows the fearless advice and loyal implementation mantra. Some public servants worry that they do not have adequate resources to collect data and facts amid a sea of disinformation and declining public trust in government.[11] Others benefit from telling ministers what they want to hear. The possibility that emails, briefing materials, and handwritten notes will be released through a freedom-of-information request means that some public servants are hesitant to provide frank advice, and so they become more covert in their dealings, such as by electing for verbal briefings over written communication. The lack of documentation compromises the collaborative nature of preparing briefs and brings into question the precision of information and institutional memory.

....
11 May, "Speaking Truth to Power Discouraged."

Loyal implementation is nuanced as well. Public servants must be politically neutral, report to government and not the opposition, follow a chain of command, and obey orders given by those with the legal authority to do so. Acting on a superior's requests must be done within the boundaries of the law, but sometimes government policy or processes are challenged.

These challenges are most acute for public servants who find themselves in a moral dilemma that strains their sense of loyalty to the government. Public servants may disagree with the government's direction. They may report their disagreement to their supervisors who may, in turn, provide advice up the chain of command to the minister (Figure 1.1). Some ministers seldom change their minds, particularly on public commitments. This leaves the public servant to choose between implementing a direction that they vehemently oppose or, if they cannot bear to proceed with the direction, finding other courses of action (described below). Without question, loyal implementation is the expectation, except in cases of legal transgression. In those instances, public servants are expected to report the misdoing to their superior or, barring that, to a whistleblower protection agency.

What recourse do public servants have when they fundamentally disagree with a political decision that is legal? For the most part, if they value their job, they must grin and bear it. A public servant who is worried about personal repercussions of speaking up will stay silent. Disobeying a request from an immediate supervisor or failing to carry out a routine job function constitute grounds for disciplinary action. This includes the possibility of being transferred and/or demoted, being asked to resign, or being fired. Those who are profoundly unhappy may avoid reprimand by requesting a reassignment to another file or position. We explore these issues in **Chapter 4.**

Tip: Recognize Government Expectations of Confidentiality
As a public institution, government takes confidentiality and secrecy extremely seriously. To understand your responsibility to protect government information, consult a code of ethics and speak with someone in human resources or an ombudsperson (an impartial investigator).

Chapter Takeaways

This chapter argues that theories of governance and public administration are important tools for public servants to preserve their proper place in the complex, dynamic world of public administration.

- Theorist Max Weber helps us appreciate the merits of hierarchy in the public service. Dispassionate organization of professionals leads to formally separating the roles of partisan and non-partisan officials in service of the government's agenda.
- These concepts coalesce into the public service bargain. It holds that public servants receive relatively generous terms of (permanent) employment in return for providing high-quality, loyal service to the (impermanent) government of the day.
- Various elements of the public service bargain fall under threat from time to time. This is acute when lines of accountability are blurred, when modes of public sector management diverge from the core principles of parliamentary democracy, when governments are preoccupied with campaign-style behaviour, or when certain benefits of employment are called into question.
- Public servants must be versed in the theoretical foundations of public administration to ensure they play an appropriate and effective role in Canadian democracy. This includes being guided by the mantra of fearless advice and loyal implementation.

CHAPTER 3

THE POLITICS OF PUBLIC POLICY

Policy is the complex set of choices that a government makes on behalf of the public. At their core, these decisions amount to defining the public interest and the best means to achieve it. But the policy direction that is obvious and appropriate to a government employee is not necessarily what the government does. A public servant's advice is just one element within many layers of formal and informal inputs that inform public policy. In this sense, policy is deeply political and involves a web of interactions infused with layers of information and perspectives. In this chapter, we delve into the politics and processes of it all.

Defining Public Policy

If politics is the practice of power, policy is its translation into action. Public policy amounts to "what government ought or ought not do, and does or does not do"[1] when shaping the economy and society. Most policy decisions involve assessing how to distribute finite resources, such as wealth, how to generate revenues, such as through taxation and fees, or how to regulate individual and group behaviour. Public policies strive to improve community, though of course there is discord about what constitutes an improvement, let alone how to accomplish it or which communities ought to benefit most. Governments' policy motivations come from many sources, as do those of their opponents. In prioritizing and defining the issues that warrant government

....

1 Dye, *Understanding Public Policy*.

attention, some are influenced by partisanship or ideology, while others are shaped by regionalism, pragmatism, convenience, or some combination of these and other factors. Effective policy-making requires extensive information and different perspectives, weighing the benefits and drawbacks of multiple options. Public servants wield considerable power in framing these trade-offs. Smooth decision-making requires a well-organized process. Some policies are reasonably straightforward and repetitive, such as administering the renewal of a licence, or establishing whether someone qualifies for a benefit. In those instances, once a policy direction is set, public servants find the most effective ways of implementing or delivering it. Other times processes are more complicated. An existing policy may suddenly require revisiting, due to evolving public preferences, or perhaps a court ruling or calamity of some sort. Health crises, natural disasters, disruptive protests, economic turmoil, and other events can force decision-makers to short-circuit the system. Sometimes ministers and their staff respond by bypassing normal procedures in the name of political expediency, with or without input from public servants. This shortcutting may be benign or opportunistic. All of this complexity makes it difficult to neatly compartmentalize how public policy is developed and refined.

Public policy usually travels along a cycle like the one in Figure 3.1. Variations of this cycle are easily located online. All have similar tenets, including the need for policy to get public and political attention as a precursor for change.

Arguably the most political of these phases is the starting point, known as *agenda-setting*. Each day, problems and solutions requiring government action are promoted by any number of political actors in any number of venues. The competition for attention highlights priority areas of concern. Political parties take policy positions; news editors and producers exercise control over what information to communicate to audiences; concerned citizens and interest groups organize protests and social media campaigns; businesses, civil society organizations, and individuals launch court challenges; watchdogs, academics, pollsters, and think tanks issue reports; other governments exert pressure; and lobbyists persuade key decision-makers behind closed doors. Within government, public servants scan the political environment and deliver

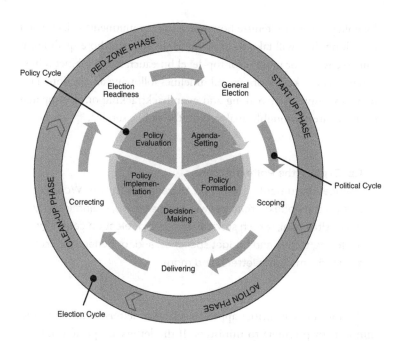

FIGURE 3.1 The Policy, Political, and Electoral Cycles

briefings. Media coverage prompts a search by decision-makers for the best way to solve the alleged public problem. Consequently, at any given time certain issues occupy the top spots on a government's list of priorities, while others, especially those not capturing public attention, are lower down the list. Public policy issues on the agenda are actively deliberated and get resources; the others must wait, perhaps indefinitely.

Just how are government agendas set? It often starts with the governing party's most recent election platform. That political document outlines the party's commitments to the electorate should it form a government. Some of the proposals were proposed and endorsed by the party membership in a policy convention and were subsequently tweaked by the leader's campaign strategists. Other proposals were designed independently by those strategists, with or without input from members of the parliamentary party caucus or other stakeholders. If public servants are fortunate, the government's platform was crafted by experienced policy experts with governance in mind and an expectation of implementation. Such platforms are often pre-assessed by policy experts to itemize how much the commitments will cost and how long they will take to implement. Even with those qualities, it can take weeks or months for top-level bureaucrats and cabinet ministers to identify key priorities and timelines following an election. This inevitably involves tweaking and even backtracking once campaign promises are thoroughly analyzed by the public service.

Tip: Explore the Poltext Archives
Political documents are prone to vanish from the Web. Try visiting the Poltext archives (www.poltext.org), maintained by Université Laval, for a historical resource of election campaign platforms, throne and budget speeches, auditor general reports, ministerial mandate letters, and more.

Major policy priorities appear in mandate letters from the prime minister (or premier) to ministers. If the letters are posted online, they constitute firm policy commitments to the public; when they are treated as cabinet confidences and are embargoed for internal use only, ministerial mandate letters signal the government's priorities to the minister, senior political staff, and senior-level public servants. Most of the content is drawn from the campaign platform, but some commitments change or emerge based on shifting political dynamics and post-election discussions with the public service. Priorities and timelines are further formalized in the government's first speech from the throne and budget speech, and in related strategic plans. In Ottawa, the throne speech is prepared by the PMO and the PCO, approved by the prime minister, and delivered by the governor general. In the provinces, the Premier's Office, Executive Council Office, premier, and lieutenant governor fulfill similar roles. Budget speeches fall under the purview of ministers of finance, advised by the finance department and other central agencies, subject to the approval of the first minister. Most public servants have limited influence over such documents, particularly given the confidential and political nature of the contents.

These documents inform the drafting of ministry business plans, also known as departmental plans. Those strategies delve into the specific priorities and actions to be pursued over the next year to five years.

Once the Treasury Board approves a business plan, each applicable minister is accountable to members of the legislature for delivering on the commitments. This accountability occurs through the tabling of policy plans in the legislature and annual budget estimates and public accounts processes, when ministers appear with their executive personnel at applicable legislative committees to defend their goals and records. Public servants further down the chain of command often develop operations plans to support these business plans. Seldom viewed by the public, these internal documents add further structure to the process of implementing the government's agenda.

> **Tip: Pay Attention to Political Declarations**
> While it is useful to be aware of the governing party's election promises, some pledges evolve, while others do not come to fruition at all. Formal declarations that are made after an election constitute a commitment to be acted upon by the government. Astute public servants pay attention to throne and budget speeches, and (if available) to ministerial mandate letters. These high-profile public statements operationalize the governing party's campaign platform by establishing what the government's immediate priorities are. They forecast what actionable requests are on the way for the public service.

Illustrated in Figure 3.2, the development and implementation of a government's agenda proceeds through several phases. Internally, deputy ministers and their executive team communicate shifts in a government's priorities to public servants. This information is publicized through public statements and annual budgets, often necessitating adjustments to business and operational plans. Changes to departmental planning are sparked by a host of factors, many of which are outside the government's direct control. Natural disasters force governments to reallocate funding and personnel to response and recovery efforts. Likewise, resource reallocation is required in the event of sudden shifts in government revenues brought about by economic downturns or upswings. Opposition parties, other governments, advocacy groups, the media, and various political

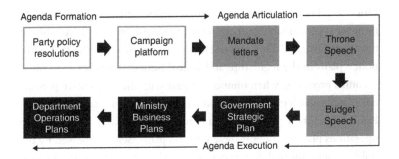

FIGURE 3.2 Operationalizing the Government's Agenda

actors may place pressure on the government to change course. The resignation of a first minister and change of government prompts an overhaul of priorities – even the words and phrases used by public servants must evolve. All told, public servants who are attuned to the broader political environment can more readily adapt to changes in the government's agenda.

Once a policy issue gets the attention of a prime minister, premier, or minister, they might want to understand their options to deal with it. They may ask public servants to gather and analyze information and to provide them with some choices of policy actions. The clerk or deputy minister are key intermediaries here. They know which public servants are best suited for analyzing policy options. Standardized processes are followed so that information is generated quickly, thoroughly, and efficiently. The policy solutions found in academic journals or trending on social media may be excellent; however, they might be idealistic or completely unworkable. Much more information from the public service is needed. Where will the money come from? What is the government's experience with this before? What are other jurisdictions doing? Who would benefit and who would suffer? Will there be different impacts on marginalized groups or regions? How is the issue playing out in the news? What do public opinion surveys say? What did the governing party's election platform say on this, if anything? What have members of other political parties said about it? Does it interfere with international commitments? These are just some of the countless political variables that factor into the process of developing policy. Some considerations are recurring and are so important that they are formally articulated in cabinet document templates, as discussed below.

A change in public policy may occur at one of several levels, depending on the magnitude of the shift.[2] Of greatest consequence, changes in directional policy entail significant, enduring commitments to radically alter the government's approach to an issue. These are typically signalled in election platforms and throne speeches. For example, a new government may opt to go in a completely different direction on addressing climate change or upholding a major spending commitment. Few policy shifts are so dramatic. Incremental changes involving a re-prioritization of objectives or a reallocation of resources to address an issue fall under the realm of strategic policy. A government may opt to increase the amount of funding to a particular department or program, for instance, or boost the number of personnel working on an issue. Just as common, a government may reduce the resources allocated to a particular policy area as a sign of its disinterest in addressing a perceived problem. Budget speeches typically outline these policy changes, which are highly political. By far the most common type of policy shifts happen at the operational level, well below the radar for most members of the public and even politicians. This is where public servants focus on smaller recalibration of existing policy tools, mechanisms, and instruments, sometimes without needing changes to legislation or even ministerial approval. Daily, public servants adjust their approaches to handling public policy challenges, ranging from where to place speed traps on roadways to whether to close or re-open businesses that have run afoul of public health regulations. It is important to bear in mind that the political executive can also choose to ignore an issue irrespective of public servants urging action.

When seeking to change the behaviour of individuals, groups, and organizations through policy, governments typically choose from a handful of common approaches. They can create disincentives, such as taxing certain behaviours or establishing regulations to curb them. Consider government approaches to alcohol, cannabis, and tobacco consumption versus the use of intravenous drugs. Alternatively, they can create incentive programs or subsidies to encourage members of the public to change how they behave. Here, retirement and children's

---

2 Hall, "Policy Paradigms, Social Learning, and the State."

educational savings programs come to mind. Governments that are averse to these carrot-and-stick approaches might instead turn to public education campaigns or nudging – a non-forced approach that changes the way people think about a particular issue. Consider how the federal government requires companies to post nutritional information on food packages so that consumers can weigh their options and potentially make healthier choices. Policy-makers can combine these approaches, creating a system of incentives, disincentives, and nudges.

Decision-making occurs once a policy is formulated. At the departmental level, a minister has the executive authority to choose what action to take, though on some matters the deputy minister may act on behalf of the minister. Some decisions require cabinet approval, such as matters that cross into multiple portfolios. The ways that political decisions occur are outlined throughout this book. This includes whether to take any action at all – recall that decisions for government to do nothing constitute public policy as well. Policy choices also include strategy. For instance, sweeping change might be unpalatable, so a series of incremental changes are introduced instead. These decisions are communicated in various ways, including press conferences, social media posts, and news releases. On occasion, unconventional ways of announcing a decision occur, such as a staffer leaking information to a journalist to float the idea and take stock of the public reaction before a final decision or official announcement is made. Alternatively, choosing to do nothing about what some allege is a problematic policy signals that the status quo is supported.

During policy implementation, government deploys resources to act on the policy decision. Success can be difficult, given the *principal-agent problem*. Also known as policy drift – and similar to the game of broken telephone – this concept holds that a directive is seldom implemented the way that decision-makers intend because it passes through so many hands. The principal is the person in charge who issues directives to agents who are tasked with carrying out orders. At each iteration, agents shift the intended course of action somewhat. So a political party that promised in the election that they would do "X" finds that by the time the policy is announced by a minister it has become "Y" and that when it is delivered it becomes "Z." Some of this reflects the layers of expertise that public servants apply to a policy idea, making adjustments that streamline, economize, or otherwise improve the outcome. But some of it is a source of considerable tension within government as various personnel negotiate the finer points of a policy initiative. A related problem is that public servants might not have the knowledge, skills, or resources to manage and deliver a government program or policy as intended.

Cabinet ministers are accountable to members of a legislature for their policy decisions. For any policy change to become law, it must pass through several stages (Figure 3.3). For a government-sponsored bill, the process ordinarily begins with a minister proposing a bill to cabinet, which is reviewed by a cabinet committee, refined in consultation with justice officials, and eventually endorsed by the cabinet. The public-facing phase of a bill begins when it is introduced to members of the legislature (first reading), debated and referred to committee for study (second reading), and voted upon by members (third reading). A federal bill must pass through all three readings in both the House of Commons and the Senate. A provincial bill must pass through just one legislative chamber, often with a lot less scrutiny than in Ottawa. The legislature's work is more focused when major policy initiatives are introduced as separate pieces of legislation. Holding the government accountable becomes more challenging when reforms are introduced in packages called omnibus bills, as legislators have less time and fewer resources to scrutinize each initiative within this larger series of proposals. At the last stage, the King's representative provides final approval of the bill through royal assent, at which point a bill becomes law.

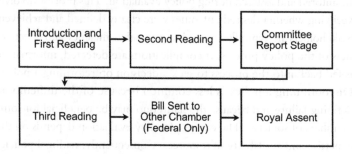

FIGURE 3.3 How a Bill Becomes a Law
Source: Senate Canada, "How a Bill Becomes a Law," accessed December 13, 2024, https://sencanada.ca/en/about/publications/how-a-bill-becomes-law/.

Policy initiatives that require government spending must pass through an additional budget process, which is commanded by central agency officials in the Department of Finance and Treasury Board. This process begins by engaging public servants and key stakeholders to determine their priorities. Based on these consultations, each department and agency submits its revenue and spending plans to the Department of Finance each fall. Later in the year, the finance minister engages in broader stakeholder and public consultations. These ideas are consolidated into a draft budget – a closely-guarded document that is discussed within cabinet, central agencies, and the highest ranks of the public service. In the spring, the finance minister announces the final version to the legislature by way of the budget speech and a budget implementation bill. Should either of these measures fail to receive approval by a majority of parliamentarians who vote on them, the government must resign. If the budget passes this test of confidence, the budget measures move to the estimates stage, where more detailed ministry spending plans are scrutinized by various parliamentary committees, whose recommendations are presented to the legislature for debate and a vote. At the end of the fiscal year, the government publishes its public accounts for further review and legislative approval. Deputy ministers play increasingly visible roles in the estimates and public accounts processes, often appearing with the minister at committee hearings. As an officer of the legislature, the auditor general is empowered to assist parliamentarians in scrutinizing the government's spending and the performance of various programs and services.

In conjunction with these spending assessments, outcomes are monitored and assessed during policy evaluation. This process involves verifying whether desired outcomes were clearly defined and achieved. Stakeholders are typically engaged to gauge the efficiency and effectiveness of the policy process. If complications are detected, information is fed back into the process to seek a decision on reforming a policy. Discontinuing a policy is less common because of the difficulty in defining failure and because the status quo may be beneficial for some members of society.[3] The extent of policy evaluation depends on the expertise and availability of resources. Consequently, national policies

....
3 Howlett, Ramesh, and Perl, *Studying Public Policy*.

are subject to formal evaluation methods involving metrics such as public opinion surveys, focus groups, and client usage data whereas small provinces can place more weight on public feedback, media reports, and political discourse. The nature of the decision-making structure within the government is another factor. Politics runs through this, too, because some cabinets are more interested in policy evaluation data than others.

Beyond the Policy Cycle

As mentioned, public policy does not operate in a compact manner. It rarely travels the cycle in an orderly fashion from one stage to the next. The cycle may start at any point. Policy-making often skips stages or moves backward in response to external forces or government direction. Thought must be given to stages later in the cycle. Ideally, the personnel involved with implementing or evaluating a policy are consulted when that policy is being formulated. That said, bear in mind that the policy cycle is an idealized process. Policy-makers should aspire to follow it even if, as with many models, this does not always reflect reality.

In fact, the notion of an orderly policy cycle is grounded in a flawed assumption that policy-makers are rational and have control over the process. Policy-makers are part of a system in which objectives are seldom well-defined. Constraints of time, funding, and expertise hinder the development of a comprehensive range of options and robust recommendations, as does the ever-changing political landscape. Data and evidence are often limited, fluctuating, or selectively used. Furthermore, direction comes from varied sources of authority. In this sort of environment public servants should treat the policy cycle as a general guide to steer the process back on course. At a minimum they can recognize and mitigate the potential pitfalls they will likely encounter.

Other times, urgent situations bypass normal processes. For instance, an ADM might be asked to draft a cabinet report overnight, without the ability to access guidance from staff. In such circumstances, the urgency of response to a situation means that policy recommendations are made without an awareness of the full scope of risks and benefits. Other cases involve considerable public pressure for the government to resolve individual circumstances, such as a sewer backup that damages basements of uninsured homeowners, or an expensive experimental drug therapy that is potentially life-saving but is not included in the provincial drug formulary. The public and media fascination with this single policy issue may become so intense that the government is unable to advance any issues without journalists pressing for a resolution. To get through this period of intense public pressure, a minister might make a policy announcement that goes against longstanding practices and is contrary to advice from public servants. This does not necessarily create a precedent. Public policy can be like a rubber band that snaps back into shape once a political crisis is over.

> **Tip: Practice Real-Time Information Monitoring**
> Setting up Google alerts about your minister, policy area, or jurisdiction can help you stay abreast of political developments. So can actively monitoring websites that aggregate news about politics and government. Considering the constraints on their time and the vastness of media platforms, senior-level officials in your organization may appreciate being kept abreast of breaking events and news stories.

Timing also determines the type of influence public servants have over the policy-making process. As illustrated in Figure 3.1, governments enter a start-up phase immediately after a general election. During this period, first ministers determine the structure and composition of their cabinets. Senior public servants help restructure the machinery of government by creating, merging, or eliminating departments. The clerk works with the first minister to assign deputy ministers to various members of cabinet, and DMs begin transition briefings to bring their ministers up to speed on the major issues in their respective portfolios. Meanwhile, public servants in central agencies work with staff in the PMO or Premier's Office to sketch out the government's legislative agenda. This scoping process often involves winnowing down dozens of campaign promises into a more manageable set of government priorities, all of which must fit within a tight cabinet and legislative calendar.

Once the governing agenda is set, public servants get to work drafting legislation, reforming government programs, and rejigging government services to help ministers deliver on their mandates. This action phase is a fertile one for innovation, with public servants having a greater opportunity to suggest new ways of doing things. During the subsequent clean-up, governments task public servants with addressing any unintended consequences or unforeseen developments lest these problems dog the party during the next campaign. Governments often shuffle their cabinets during this period, requiring public servants to undertake another round of ministerial transition briefings (**Chapter 4**). In the final year before the election, the government enters a red zone: a period of making good news announcements and trying to avoid unpopular decisions. Some major policy decisions may be made in later years of a mandate if they are expected to be popular, fulfill an outstanding commitment, or represent a wedge issue to set the governing party's approach apart from the opposition. The government's final budget serves as the centrepiece of its re-election campaign, and meaningful public servant input into it can help make post-election implementation that much easier.

Briefing Effectively

By now it should be evident that providing the right kind of information to the right audiences at the right time is crucial to effective policy-making. Each government establishes and continuously revamps its internal briefing processes to ensure this happens as efficiently as possible. From file-naming and storage protocols to project and approvals management systems to forms and templates – public servants are inundated with constantly changing rules for how to communicate their advice to decision-makers. Certain principles and practices for effective briefing are timeless, however.

Policy-makers expect public servants to deliver non-partisan policy guidance based on a review of information and consultations with stakeholders. Good research, strong writing, and attention to detail are essential. Information must be presented objectively and clearly, and authors often need to deliver relevant details promptly. To maximize efficiency and the approvals process, authors of briefing documents must strictly adhere to a standardized format. Ministers and their staff routinely review hundreds of policy documents, and they must know how and where to find the right kinds of details in hurried circumstances. There are many templates and instruments in government for compiling information in a succinct, consistent manner.

Major shifts in policy at the directional or strategic level must flow through the centre of government. In federal and provincial governments, decisions on whether to pursue a new policy approach or establish a major new program, service, or other initiative often proceed through a *memorandum to cabinet* (or cabinet report). So, too, do policy decisions required by law to receive cabinet approval. A cabinet submission is a succinct analysis of a policy issue that recommends a course of action to ministers. Supporting materials lay out the following: the rationale for the recommendation and reasons for rejecting other options; the costs, benefits, and risks involved; any alignment with relevant legislation, government commitments, and intergovernmental agreements; and high-level plans for implementing and communicating the policy change. Various lenses may be applied, such as sections that identify the implications for rural areas or which perform a gender-based analysis. A memorandum to cabinet is typically drafted by policy analysts and reviewed by more senior bureaucrats before being handed off to political staff within the lead departments. Throughout the process, central agency personnel guide the proposal to ensure it aligns with the government's commitments and priorities. In this sense, cabinet submissions provide advice to ministers who consider the document's information during cabinet meetings or committees, as well as serve as consensus documents among different ministries, political and non-partisan staff, and line departments and the centre.

Most strategic policy recommendations are also reviewed by the Treasury Board. Submissions to this special standing committee of ministers provide finer details about the design, delivery, and implementation of the policy change. Public servants must fully cost their proposal and produce comprehensive implementation, evaluation, and risk-management plans. If approved by the Treasury Board, the policy must proceed to full cabinet for endorsement and the legislature for approval of any spending.

At the operational level, most policy recommendations are conveyed by way of a *briefing note*: a tightly written summary that succinctly informs the reader about the issue at hand, why they should take it seriously, and what they should do about it. A briefing note might request a decision or prepare for an event or situation. Briefing notes and their variants (e.g., information notes, synopses, and so on) are a means of conveying potentially complex information in a digestible manner. They are prepared for busy executives who do not have time to read up about an issue and need to quickly become familiar with the most pertinent details. The author seeks to present as much useful information as possible within very tight space constraints. This must be done in a reader-friendly manner that informs as well as enlightens. Summarizing an issue in a page or two with minimal jargon and acronyms is challenging for most public servants, particularly for subject matter experts used to writing at length about their areas of expertise. Decision-makers value briefings that are concise and easy to understand, yet comprehensive, forceful, analytical, and, above all, actionable. In short, an excellent briefing note anticipates and answers all major questions surrounding the issue at hand and presents it in the clearest, most efficient way possible (Table 3.1).

All told, public servants must consider a multitude of considerations when crafting effective briefing materials. The amount and availability of information have grown exponentially in recent decades, first with the advent of websites, and then with the emergence of social media, big data, and artificial intelligence (AI). So, too, have the expectations from decision-makers who insist that the public service provide them with the most comprehensive and up-to-date information available. Today's public servant has more data at their disposal than ever before, resulting in an exponential improvement in analytical advice. Yet, public servants must be cautious. Information disorder persists throughout the online world, exposing public servants to misleading and fabricated content.[4] Like all digital citizens, public servants are part of their own, often insular, online communities. These echo chambers

....
4 Wardle and Derakhshan, *Information Disorder.*

TABLE 3.1 Government of Canada Briefing Note "Dos and Don'ts"

BRIEFING NOTE DOS	BRIEFING NOTE DON'TS
Audience	
• Know your reader's perspective and concerns. • Anticipate and answer your reader's questions.	• Don't assume that your reader has the same technical knowledge as you do.
Style	
• Keep it short: 2 pages maximum. • Be clear and concise: write sentences averaging 15–20 words up to a maximum of 30 words; write paragraphs of no more than 5–6 sentences, or 7–9 lines. • Use the active voice and action verbs.	• Don't use too many acronyms or abbreviations. • Stay away from jargon and technical terms (define them if you have to use them). • Avoid strings of nouns. • Avoid using too many adverbs and adjectives.
Organization and Structure	
• Get to the point quickly: present the most important information first (giving general information before specific). • Put the right information in the right section. • Present your rationale clearly and logically. • Present information in small and manageable chunks: use bullets and tables when needed. • Use appendices for details, but don't overdo it.	• Don't include more than one idea for each paragraph. • Don't introduce new elements or repeat information in the conclusion and recommendations.
Content	
• Be clear on the issue of the briefing note. • Summarize what you want the reader to grasp quickly. • Provide pertinent and complete information based on objective analysis and consultations. • Make clear recommendations linked to facts. • State possible consequences when applicable.	• Don't use ambiguous statements or vague timelines. • Don't hide or diminish the seriousness of a problem or situation. • Avoid presenting unsubstantiated arguments. • Refrain from giving your personal opinions: stick to concrete facts. • Don't overwhelm your reader with details.

(Continued)

TABLE 3.1 Continued

BRIEFING NOTE DOS	BRIEFING NOTE DON'TS
Process	
• Make a plan and focus on the core issue: aim for quality arguments, not quantity of information.	• Don't write before you are clear on the objective of the request.
• Check all the facts.	• Don't start writing the summary before you finish writing the content of the briefing note.
• Be discerning when copying and pasting.	
• Discuss the proposed changes with the editors.	• Limit the number of changes made for reasons of style and personal preference.
• Learn from previous briefing notes.	

Source: Translation Bureau, Public Works and Government Services Canada, "Write Clear and Effective Briefing Notes," September 27, 2022, https://www.noslangues-ourlanguages.gc.ca/en/writing-tips-plus/clear-communication-write-clear-and-effective-briefing-notes.

may isolate them from alternative viewpoints and give them a false sense of social reality when identifying policy problems and options.

Generative artificial intelligence presents public servants with both opportunities and challenges.[5] AI chatbots can boost productivity by acting as an e-government interface and by serving as virtual research assistants. Generative AI can serve as a brainstorming tool, translate large swaths of text into another language, and enhance the clarity of bureaucratic writing. It can compile comprehensive and increasingly accurate bodies of literature, producing reviews in a fraction of the time it would take a human. Manual processes ranging from computer coding to paperwork can be automated to streamline processes, accelerate timelines, and improve productivity. Quantitative data analysis and predictive analytics hold much promise, particularly with the large amount of data now being compiled by government agents. Removing standard human bias from the recommendations process may also provide a more objective outcome, at least on the surface.

Even so, AI tools are only as effective as the data and coding upon which they are built. Content generated by AI is compiled from the Internet, and without proper attribution there is a risk of plagiarism. Moreover, artificial intelligence is prone to fabricating information

....

5 Auld, Casovan, Clarke, and Faveri, "Governing AI Through Ethical Standards."

and presenting falsehoods as facts that go undetected by non-experts – a potential hazard to public policy decision-making and a source of considerable public embarrassment. Predominant cultural, ethnic, gender, and other biases are integrated into most AI models, forcing public servants to consider the extent to which AI helps meet their governments' commitments to diversity in policy-making. Its use raises important ethical considerations, particularly around the concept of accountability. If decision-makers come to rely on artificial intelligence for recommendations or even decisions, questions arise as to how to safeguard public privacy, who is responsible for wrongdoing, and the role of public servants in the future. Moreover, used improperly, AI has the potential to erode trust in the advice provided by public servants, which would have serious repercussions for the integrity of the public service bargain.

With these benefits and drawbacks in mind, governments are developing and refining guidelines for public servants on the use of generative AI in the workplace. These practices typically centre on protecting citizens' privacy with respect to uploading personal information and on transparency when using the tools. The rapid pace of AI development places the onus on public servants to self-educate about both the considerable opportunities and potential pitfalls.

Tip: Discuss Internal Policy about Using AI
Artificial Intelligence tools are changing the way government works. They can quickly distill complex bureaucratic writing into key messages and talking points. They can be used to analyze and visualize data, to power e-government chatbots that answer the public's questions, and to run policy simulations. However, there are pitfalls. Submitting internal information to an AI interface could violate confidentiality rules, and AI platforms are notorious for inaccuracies and creating misleading information. Check about internal policies on the use of generative AI.

Whatever the source, even the best empirical evidence may not convince decision-makers about a course of action. As highlighted throughout this book, a public servant's role is to offer candid advice grounded in their specialized expertise. Senior personnel on both sides of the political-bureaucratic divide must weigh multiple considerations when deciding what action to recommend to ministers. Sometimes this means going with another department or agency's suggestions or prioritizing a different policy. Ministers have their own sources of influence. A public servant's advice might well be the most efficient and effective in policy terms, but it might be unpalatable politically. Following a recommended course of action could damage the governing party's reputation with other governments, or it might outrage certain members of its caucus, voter base, or donors. Occasionally, governments side with populist forces that prefer policies that originate from non-expert sources. These political calculations weigh heavily on politicians and political staff as they determine what is in the public interest. To ensure that professional advice is taken seriously, public servants must understand the politics of public policy and public administration without succumbing to partisanship. That is the topic of the next chapter.

Chapter Takeaways

This chapter illustrates that public servants must be attuned to the politics of the policy-making process.

- Policy involves the translation of power into action. Understanding the power dynamics within the broader political system is a prerequisite for identifying and resolving policy problems.
- The policy cycle is a general guide for understanding how policy is developed and implemented. A more accurate picture emerges when you consider how seldom your work conforms to these categories. Public servants should strive to guide the process back in line.
- Public servants must be attuned to the political rhythms of their jurisdiction. Election cycles in particular have fast and slow periods when it comes to the development of new policy directions.
- Heads of government, cabinet ministers, and their political staff need clearly written information summaries. Internal templates for briefing notes and cabinet submissions are used to optimize efficiency, consistency, and comprehension.

- Policy-makers consider an array of information when making decisions. Only a fraction of this comes from public servants. Political decisions therefore may or may not align with the advice provided in briefing notes or cabinet documents.

CHAPTER 4

THE POLITICS OF PUBLIC ADMINISTRATION

Our opening chapters established the basic tenets of politics and governance in Canada. For the most part, the Canadian constitution and the laws that flow from it act as guideposts between which the public, bureaucrats, journalists, parliamentarians, Indigenous leaders, first ministers, and others must operate. This chapter explores the space between those guideposts. It reveals just how murky the rules of public administration can be.

Accountability and Centralization

Delivering on a government's agenda requires a firm sense of who is accountable to whom and for what. In **Chapter 1**, we discussed how responsible government holds cabinet accountable to the legislature through the concept of confidence. We mentioned that individual ministers are accountable to the rest of cabinet for delivering on agreed-upon priorities. In addition, Canada's form of representative democracy holds individual parliamentarians accountable to their constituents through elections. Furthermore, party leaders are held to account by caucus and party members, as well as their opponents. Voters pass judgment on governments and politicians through these indirect ways.

Accountability is a more complicated concept within the bureaucracy itself. In a strict sense, accountability ought to be confined to the relationship between ministers and the legislature. In a broader sense, many public service organizations have adopted the term as one of their core ethical principles.

Ask public servants to whom they are accountable, and you are likely to hear a range of responses. Some might reply that they work for their respective ministers. Others view their relationship with their direct supervisors as taking precedence. Some believe they are employed by the general public because the title of their vocation implies serving the public good, while fiduciary thinking and political rhetoric can lead them to feel a duty to taxpayers. Still others maintain that they report to the premier or prime minister or perhaps the Crown. Ultimately, to varying degrees, all of these answers are valid. The broad concept of accountability requires public servants to balance their responsibilities according to their own sense of priorities and ethics.

There is an important distinction between the broader concept of accountability and the narrower notion of answerability. Accountability requires ministers and public servants to carry out responsibilities they are assigned by law or policy. Otherwise, they face personal or professional consequences. The principle of ministerial responsibility is grounded in this notion of accountability. By the same token, public servants are held directly responsible for poor performance and negligence through disciplinary mechanism. They are accountable for their actions if they fail to live up to their contractual obligations. On the other hand, according to the PCO, answerability involves "a duty to inform and explain, but does not include the personal consequences associated with accountability."[1] Deputy ministers may be called to testify before parliamentary committees to answer for the goings-on in their departments, for instance. Yet, it is the minister who is accountable to both the first minister and the legislature for the ministry's performance.

The concentration of power in various parts of each public service is driven by this concept of accountability. Obligation flows upward to the top of organizational hierarchies and inward to the centre of government and each ministry. Prime ministers and premiers wield considerable power over ministers, for instance. They choose who to appoint, promote, demote, and remove from cabinet, which gives them authority to define and oversee the government's agenda. They amass talent in their central agencies and consolidate top staff

....

[1] Privy Council Office, *Guidance for Deputy Ministers*.

in political positions within the Prime Minister's Office or Premier's Office. From time to time, first ministers place former political staff in the non-partisan centre of government, including the Executive or Privy Council Office and Treasury Board Secretariat. As discussed in **Chapter 1**, the clerk heads the Executive/Privy Council Office and is the highest-ranking public servant. The clerk is the chief deputy minister and provides advice to the first minister. This includes overseeing the cadre of deputy ministers that serve the remaining members of cabinet. All of those senior public servants serve in their roles at the discretion of the government led by the prime minister or premier.

Individual ministers take a comparable approach within their respective domains. Ministers often create similar central bodies within their own departments. Deputy ministers may assemble policy coordination, human resources, and communications units within departments. This mirrors the central agencies found in Executive/Privy Council Offices. Deputies clarify shifts in the government's agenda and priorities for all employees of the department. They help staff understand how these policy directions align with the departmental mandate and the roles of various employees. Accountable to ministers in similar ways for major decisions, heads of *agencies, boards, and commissions* (ABCs) also centralize control within their offices. Many appointees on the boards of ABCs are affiliated with the governing party. For the most part, these arm's-length organizations run their day-to-day affairs without political oversight, although their mandates and budgets are subject to ministerial approval.

This dual consolidation of power – at the centre of government and at the top of the hierarchy of each department or ABC – sets up a system of intragovernmental relations. Elites at the head of their respective organizations coordinate joint business. Ministers interact with each other around the cabinet table and in committees, just as deputy ministers meet regularly to discuss areas of common cause and interest.

In this sense, employees of the federal and provincial governments may view the consolidation of power within the bureaucracy through two overlapping perspectives. They see that control over the government agenda is concentrated in the centre of government. Influence over their minister's agenda is similarly concentrated within their own minister's and deputy minister's offices. Within this system, a public servant's ability to shape directions and outcomes is constrained. It may feel like the public service is stranded in the valleys between the peaks of power atop each ministry. Supervisors have limited capacity or authority to share information or to communicate advice both up and down the hierarchy. At times, it can be challenging to convey fearless advice while remaining open with staff and/or to ensure loyal implementation of political decisions.

The Structure and Machinery of Government

Federal and provincial governments in Canada feature three separate branches (executive, legislative, and judicial), many ministries, and a stable bureaucracy. All of these governments look different, even if they share similar structures, and how they are organized can change rapidly and repeatedly over a short period of time. Changes of government following an election are the most obvious catalysts for restructuring. A new party in power and a new executive are likely to reshape government based on their ideological approach or platform commitments. The first minister and cabinet decide how government should be organized, often with advice from the Privy Council or Executive Council Office. The number and names of ministries vary. For example, parties on the political left are likely to have stand-alone labour ministries, while parties on the political right may roll those functions under economic development. Sometimes a cabinet shuffle shifts ministers to new portfolios and/or ministers are added to or removed from cabinet. Other times, a shuffle involves creating, dissolving, renaming, combining, or splitting ministries. Considerable reorganizing also occurs when the governing party replaces its leader, resulting in a new head of government without a general election.

Prime ministers and premiers undertake mid-term cabinet shuffles for various reasons. This reorganization often involves demoting underperformers, promoting effective ministers, and introducing loyalists into key positions. They may seek to emphasize specific areas of government business, such as creating a new department to tackle a pressing issue or appointing a talented minister to manage a challenging portfolio. Additionally, maintaining internal party balance can be a factor. When a minister chooses to retire from politics, the prime minister or premier may appoint an existing minister to temporarily fill the vacancy while planning a broader cabinet shuffle.

Amid these changes, clerks have distinct considerations to consider when managing their teams of deputies. Clerks make recommendations to first ministers about who should be appointed as deputy ministers, decisions that are confirmed by cabinets. Deputy ministers often stay on with their departments to ease the transition of new ministers into their roles following a change in government or cabinet shuffle. After this transition period, many of them are moved to new positions within government. They provide a new lens on a portfolio, bring fresh energy and enthusiasm to their new role, or perhaps have a better personal or professional fit with another minister. Other times they are dismissed from government and thanked for their service. Deputy minister reassignments may occur independently from cabinet shuffles when clerks manage their workforces to implement the government's directions. Changes in the senior ranks of the public service take on different flavours from jurisdiction to jurisdiction. Public servants should be prepared for routine work to decelerate as new leaders transition into their roles.[2]

A similar slowdown occurs as governments enter *caretaker mode* around general elections. During these periods, which can stretch over months before and after the election, major policy changes are put on hold so as not to bind the next government or advance policies without a democratically elected legislature to oversee them. Senior public servants shift into maintenance or stewardship mode while they await the incoming cabinet.[3] It is wise during this time to talk to seasoned public servants in your area. Their experiences can provide context for what's to come and the implications for public administration.

Political Acumen

In these ways, governing is a political process. Yet, the bureaucracy must stay out of the partisan fray. It must offer impartial advice to the

2 Althaus and Vakil, "Political Transitions."
3 Brock and Bowden, "Beyond the Writ."

government of the day regardless of the people and party in power, and irrespective of a public servant's personal views of those partisans. Public servants are expected to present the best available options within the parameters of the elected government's priorities. They must provide advice that is consistent with available data and the governing principles articulated by the government. Without evidence, the advice borders on partisan hackery; yet, without attention to political objectives, it risks being unresponsive to the directions of the democratically elected politicians in charge of the government. Once directions are issued, public servants must set aside any personal dissonance to provide the most effective service possible.

To excel, the public service must be attuned to politics and ideology. Here, we must recognize the difference between politics and partisanship. Public servants are expected to be non-partisan while working for government. That is, they should not openly advocate for the interests of any political party or political ideology during their day-to-day work. Their job is not to help the governing party get re-elected, nor is it to undermine that party; rather, a public servant is tasked with ensuring the government, regardless of its partisan flavour, is in the best position possible to implement its chosen agenda. To accomplish this, many public servants are expected to be politically astute. They should apply their knowledge of the political environment to provide the best advice and service in the achievement of government goals. Therefore, public servants need a solid understanding of the political system in which they operate.

> **Tip: Participate in Public Service Networking Opportunities**
> Consider joining a public service organization like the Institute of Public Administration of Canada. IPAC and its regional groups host networking events and lifelong learning seminars on topics relevant to public servants. Getting involved in your labour union can also be a forum for networking.

Effective public servants are astute and agile, prudent and tactful, principled and ethical. They possess what's known as *political acumen*, which involves an ability to apply knowledge of the political system to work effectively with colleagues, stakeholders, and decision-makers in accomplishing government objectives. Acumen requires understanding the unique and oft-changing interests of ministers and senior bureaucrats, as well as those of various stakeholders and the broader public. It means working with partners across one's own department and in other parts of the bureaucracy to generate consensus around how to advance the government's agenda. Broadly speaking, political acumen amounts to the intersection of four key elements:

- broad knowledge of internal and external power structures, both within and across governments;
- refined situational awareness when it comes to the political, economic, and social environment;
- soft skills in diplomacy, including strong emotional and social intelligence, and skills in persuasion and collaborative negotiation; and
- a firm ethical foundation, grounded in the values of the public service.

Knowledge of Power

Discussed at length in this book, power in government is concentrated at the centre of each organization and at the top of the organizational chart. Astute public servants appreciate that subtle dynamics exist between branches of government, bureaucrats, and their political masters, inside individual ministries, and among different jurisdictions. Indeed, power is distributed among governments in Canada. Few policy areas are confined to a single jurisdiction. The concentration at the top of each organization helps with coordination while limiting the influence of any single public servant.

First ministers' meetings sit at the apex of this system. The prime minister and provincial/territorial premiers periodically meet with one another to discuss common matters. Conferences involving multiple first ministers are held to generate consensus on pan-Canadian issues like health care and climate change. The premiers meet twice a year without the prime minister, as the Council of the Federation. These forums are an opportunity for collaboration on economic, social, and environmental issues and to pressure the federal government. The prime minister periodically convenes a meeting of all first ministers.

By far the most visible, these summits are only some of many avenues within Canada's system of intergovernmental bodies.

Federal, provincial, and territorial (FPT) ministers meet regularly with their counterparts to tackle common challenges and share best practices. Separate meetings of justice, health, social services, education, environment, natural resources, finance, and other ministers take place throughout each year. On occasion, these meetings involve Indigenous leaders. An expansive field of bureaucracy has grown within each jurisdiction to support Canada's complex web of intergovernmental relations. Deputy ministers must collaborate to prepare for meetings of premiers and ministers. Below them, public servants hold video meetings to stay abreast of the goings-on in their policy areas. Hundreds of hours of bureaucratic preparations go into every summit involving a group of ministers from across Canada.

Situational Awareness

Public servants should understand the complex, ever-changing world around them. As a government employee, you must have a good radar to pick up on all of the political, economic, and social influences on your work – and an even better filter to determine the most important pieces of intelligence amid all that information. In other words, you want to catch everything but be selective in what you retain and use.

This information is crucial in determining whether the window is open or closed for policy innovation.[4] Adept public servants will both see and anticipate the opportunities that emerge only when a problem becomes salient enough and the political will to do something about it accumulates. Having the right solution precisely when politicians are looking for one is key to achieving policy change. At times, public servants can help shift or expand the policy window, opening decision-makers' minds to a new set of options by alerting members of their teams and their supervisors to the problem or solution, building credibility and resources. Doing all of this requires a firm understanding of the ever-changing political environment around them.

....
4 Kingdon, *Agendas, Alternatives, and Public Policies.*

As discussed in **Chapter 3**, public servants must be attuned to the political goings-on in their jurisdiction, if only because of how politics has an impact on the policy cycle and timing of major government initiatives. Politicians may open and close windows of opportunity as quickly as the popularity of governments wax and wane. Public servants need to be aware of political undercurrents to anticipate challenges and tensions and be responsive at critical times. Most good ideas don't get shelved; they just await the right opportunity. When the conditions align to advance policy innovation, a public servant needs to be ready with previous studies, data, and practical ideas to catch the moment. A prepared public servant can make an enormous contribution at the appropriate time. Advancing some policy files means playing a long game and possibly waiting until there is a change of government. Periodically the right combination of leadership, resources, and public interest will result in significant progress being made on a particular topic.

Paying attention to multiple sources of media will equip you with awareness of current events. Being politically aware means more than following opinion polls, reading headlines, listening to podcasts, following social media, or watching question period. Political tremors are much subtler and require ears to the ground. As discussed above, you should pay attention to the power dynamics within governments to assess your leaders' room to manoeuvre. A rift between ministers or a chasm between cabinet and the backbench is often weeks old by the time it hits the media. This lag can have an impact on the timing and reception of advice. Political divisions among deputy ministers or other senior bureaucrats are unlikely to surface publicly. Yet, such internal conflict will have an impact on the decision-making calculus further up the hierarchy.

Tip: Incorporate Social Media into Environmental Scans
Understanding changes in public sentiment, identifying emerging issues, and staying ahead of misinformation are all important. Governments incorporate social media into their daily news-monitoring scans. You can enhance these searches by using tools like Hootsuite, Brandwatch, or Mention to track and analyze conversations in your policy area. Ensure you monitor a variety of platforms, including niche forums or blogs, and set notifications for posts from influencers and thought leaders.

Public servants need to also be aware of Indigenous politics and governance in their region. This includes knowledge about treaties, unceded territories, and Indigenous rights, both contemporary and historical. Public servants also need to sustain their situational awareness by paying attention to developments in the rest of Canada, as well as applicable global happenings. This involves looking beyond monitoring information reported in the news or posts on social media to perusing the news release sections of websites of other departments and governments.

Awareness of political happenings includes familiarity with economic developments. Governments have limited control over the fate of their economies. Thus, in most cases a public servant staying abreast of global economic trends is not useful from a utilitarian perspective. That said, economies have a direct impact on government budgets. A downturn typically results in calls for spending restraint. Austerity can vary from funding freezes or spending cutbacks to public servant attrition, even layoffs. Economic upswings or downturns may prompt pressure for increased government spending. A spendthrift administration opens opportunities for new or expanded government programs and services. Either scenario could be a catalyst for public sector innovation, the former driven by efficiency, the latter by enhanced capacity. This is why public servants are wise to brush up on basic macroeconomic theory and the principles of public finance.

A bigger challenge is ensuring that people in executive offices are aware of insights from front-line workers who engage with the public and/or who are involved with implementing policy. Senior decision-makers in government can be disconnected from the expertise and experiences of lower-ranking public servants who are directly involved in operations and services. Equally, the satisfaction of the clients of government programs and services are not always considered. Having a service-oriented approach to policy can help remedy these gaps.

Finally, be aware of social influences. Many public servants are at least partially motivated by the prospect of improving the lives of current and future generations. Doing so requires an in-depth understanding of the broader population. Staying abreast of demographic trends through Statistics Canada updates is part of this. To frame their work and provide the best advice to policy-makers, public servants should know whether a population is growing or shrinking, aging or getting younger, becoming more or less diverse, and so on. More than this, they need to be attuned to social-cultural trends in society. Generational shifts have an impact on public demands on government.

Soft Skills

Leveraging knowledge and situational awareness requires a high level of social intelligence and strong soft skills. Hard skills are focused techniques, such as effective writing or quantitative analysis, that are refined through advanced training. Soft skills encompass communication, teamwork, problem-solving, consensus-building, and other attributes that are needed for a productive working relationship with co-workers. These talents enable a public servant to interact positively with ministers, deputies, political staff, colleagues, stakeholders, and the public. Soft skills involve compiling and then applying intelligence about one's social environment. They enable planning and executing an effective strategy to bring others onside, if not on board, with your approach to delivering on the government's direction.

Not everyone in the public service operates in a co-operative way. Competitiveness and obstruction exist. Morale can be weak for any number of reasons. Public servants are increasingly expected to contribute to a respectful workplace that is devoid of bullying, promotes excellent mental health, advances equitable practices, and provides a safe environment free from harassment. This concept of collaboration corresponds well with the consensus-building required of many public service roles.

Co-operation is a challenging process. Political actors seldom desire the same outcome for the same reasons. Building consensus starts with defining a common set of principles to abide by and objectives to pursue. It proceeds to generating commitments among partners to pursue those outcomes jointly, to the benefit of everyone involved. In this way, consensus is not the same as compromise or concession. It requires more strength, perseverance, and talent to collaborate and reach consensus than it does to compete and achieve accommodation.

Ethics of Public Service

It is not enough to know how power works and how to use it. Ethics matter. Without moral moorings, politicians and public servants may be tempted to use their knowledge of power structures and their persuasion skills to take advantage of their privileged role for personal gain. Unprincipled behaviour will earn a reputation for slickness but not acuity, no matter how smart or talented you are. Fortunately, unscrupulous behaviour is rare.

Most public service organizations in Canada are guided by written ethics codes. These rules define the bounds of acceptable behaviour and are embedded in each public servant's terms of employment. Acting unethically could therefore result in disciplinary action or termination. Even in the absence of formal sanction, failure to abide by ethical principles will result in a loss of trust from colleagues. Without this credibility, no amount of know-how or talent will help a public servant to succeed in an interconnected and collaborative organization like government.

Formal codes of conduct provide only broad guidelines for most difficult ethical dilemmas, however. What if a backbench member of the legislature calls your office to request information about a sensitive internal issue? What do you do when a political staffer asks for a briefing note you are drafting and wants to edit it? What if you are providing support to a minister as part of a travelling delegation, and they insist on taking their formal briefings late in the evening, at the hotel lounge? Beyond applying broad principles such as transparency, honesty, integrity, and the like, public servants must weigh their personal values and professional goals against their legal and constitutional obligations.[5]

Ethical tensions in the public service are longstanding, as a federal task force chaired by deputy minister John Tait in the 1990s uncovered.[6] Public servants reported conflicts between their responsibility to provide stability in programs and services while being accountable for innovative results. They grappled with a desire to serve the public good while loyally implementing government directions that fell short of meeting the public's needs. They cited downsizing and

5 Kernaghan and Langford, *The Responsible Public Servant*.
6 Tait, "A Strong Foundation."

cutbacks as significant barriers to success. Reading the Tait Report may provide today's public servants with the solace that the challenges they face are not unique to their generation. It remains an excellent discussion guide for individuals and teams. This said, the report's lack of firm recommendations is of little comfort to those seeking concrete solutions to these ethical tensions. Governments across Canada have developed or refined ethics codes in the decades since that report. The broad guidelines for behaviour are open to interpretation by public sector employees and managers. This ethical ambiguity allows flexibility to address incidents on a case-by-case basis. The murkiness can be discomforting for those in the midst of a dilemma.

All of this illustrates that discretion is warranted with respect to loyal implementation. Requests to take action that would go outside of the rules established in law or employment guidelines are problematic. Fudging the numbers in a public report is unacceptable. So is hiring someone based on their personal or partisan relationship with the minister. Other situations are muddier. If your minister's office insists you rejig a funding formula to ensure that a specific community, known to be in a swing riding, receives more infrastructure dollars, it should give you reason for pause. Deleting emails or shredding documents in anticipation of the content being made publicly available through access to information is clearly deceptive in light of freedom-of-information laws. In fact, doing so can result in criminal conviction and imprisonment. Yet a public servant does not have the executive authority to overrule a minister or senior political staff. What should be done? A simple test is to note whether instructions are contrary to the law. If so, a public servant is obligated not to participate and must inform a supervisor. If something seems dubious or even unethical, but it is legal, the norm is to faithfully implement the decisions. Exercise caution: request instructions in writing; review your public service code of ethics and values; confer with co-workers and superiors; and anticipate that public servants occupying a higher position will uphold the public service bargain. This requires faith that the system is designed to hold the government accountable. Whatever your position, you retain legal rights and personal moral standards.

An extreme option for an alarmed employee is to leak the alleged transgression to entities outside the public service, such as a journalist or the opposition. Depending on the nature of the leak, this may result in grounds for dismissal, fines, or even criminal charges. At the very least, revealing government information would contravene the *Public Service Act* or equivalent. The rare practice of government leaks highlights the extent to which certain public servants, under certain circumstances, (mis)interpret their democratic responsibility. They may perceive government action or unwillingness to act as a direct threat to lives or livelihoods, for example. This may compel them to release information in an effort to prevent more damage or to allow others to hold the government to account for wrongdoing. From a less altruistic perspective, leaks may be evidence of unethical and arrogant actions by public servants who substitute their own judgment about the public interest for that of a democratically elected government. Leaking is an extreme course of action that rarely warrants considering. This is especially true in jurisdictions with strong whistleblowing laws, which allow public servants to report misdeeds without risking their positions. The day-to-day functioning of government, however, and Canadians' confidence in it, requires the type of loyalty embedded in the public service bargain (**Chapter 2**).

The Merit Principle

That same bargain provides security for public servants in terms of their employment. As Weber recommended, government hiring managers are tasked with staffing a qualified and competent public service. Modern public services, like those in Canada, recruit non-partisan employees using the *merit principle*. This means that most government jobs are open to competition. Positions are awarded to the most competent, qualified applicants based on an impartial and transparent set of employment standards and practices that are followed by a team of public servants (see Box 4.1). Job competitions are adjudicated by an independent body (e.g., a public service commission) that is insulated from political pressure. The merit principle extends beyond government hiring to include the awarding of government contracts through tendering processes.

BOX 4.1 STAGES OF HIRING IN THE MERIT SYSTEM

1. Need identified and authorized
2. Hiring committee formed and job ad created (includes role, duties, skills, pay, deadline, commitment to employment equity)
3. HR reviews and posts ad (internally or externally)
4. Applications reviewed and shortlisted (by HR, hiring manager, and/or committee)
5. Interviews conducted (standard questions for all)
6. Testing or second interview (if needed)
7. Candidates ranked and selected
8. References and background check
9. Hiring recommendation formalized
10. Job offer extended (with terms and start date)
11. Orientation and onboarding

That is the ideal. However, there are variations. One notable deviation is that some public sector positions are not open to the broader public. Governments confine competitions to Canadian citizens or existing public servants, particularly in times of fiscal restraint. Hiring priorities include public servants who are on a leave of absence or laid off, employees who have been informed that their position will be eliminated, and certain employees who were medically discharged. These and other principles, like respecting seniority, are built into many collective bargaining agreements. Hiring managers may craft positions to secure or retain specific individuals, closing off consideration of other qualified applicants. Whether intentional or subconscious, this type of favouritism has advantages, such as talent recruitment and retention, and disadvantages, such as low morale and a lack of new ways of thinking. To further limit bias in hiring, name-blind techniques can be used, whereby the names of candidates are obscured during the screening process. Unconscious bias training can go some way to helping public servants recognize and traverse these fault lines.

Another variation is that hiring managers often rely on their sense of how well each candidate would fit into the existing team. Personality, unique qualities and talents, and other intangible attributes can figure into this subjective part of the decision-making process when top candidates are otherwise equal. A further challenge to the ideals of the merit principle is that an incumbent who has been filling a position on an interim or acting basis may have the inside track when the job is publicly advertised.

Tip: Chat with an HR Manager about Hiring Practices
Many hiring managers are willing to give you an insider's take on the hiring process. Consider approaching a human resource professional for more information about recruitment and hiring policies. This is particularly useful if you seek information about a specific field.

The merit principle is only one factor in employment decisions. This is particularly true as you advance higher up the organization and as you move outward to arm's-length government bodies. For example, some high-level and central agency appointments are based on perceived loyalty or alignment with the values and priorities of the government of the day. In those instances, the office of a prime minister, premier, or minister may take a hands-on approach to selecting the public servants they trust most to implement the government's agenda. In other circumstances a search prioritizes the ability of a candidate to demonstrate an absence of loyalty to any party and exhibit no predisposition in values. What matters is the individual's reputation for making things happen, getting decisions implemented, and helping a minister navigate the complexities of governing. For these reasons many top public service positions are exempt from rules and legislation governing hiring practices.

In addition, public service hiring often pursue employment equity goals. Public sector managers must demonstrate efforts to recruit Canadians from underrepresented groups. This is necessary to build a diverse and representative bureaucracy that resembles the citizenry it serves. As of 2025, federal *Employment Equity Act* requires that "special measures" be taken to address employment disadvantages and the reasonable "accommodation of differences" of women, people with disabilities, Indigenous Peoples, and members of visible minority communities.[7] Provinces and territories often define similar categories for diversity, equity, and inclusion in the public service. These aims are not designed to conflict with the merit principle that the most competent and qualified candidate gets the job. Rather, they ensure that members of traditionally marginalized groups do not have their merit discounted by virtue of who they are.

Canada's employment equity practices differ from the affirmative action found in the United States. There, public sector employers use preferential treatment to meet hard quotas in terms of new hires. In Canada, targets are established and recruitment is broadened. However, for the most part, during the hiring process a candidate's personal characteristics may not be considered. Exceptions involve positions where a person's lived experience brings value to the role. For instance, Indigenous Peoples may demonstrate a greater capacity to fulfill the duties of an Indigenous relations position because of their familiarity with cultural and community norms. Other roles may require cultural sensitivity and language proficiency, by virtue of dealing with a particular group of stakeholders or clients. Findings of discrimination and racism within the public service that have an impact on the career progression of Indigenous, Black, and racialized employees suggest that more needs to be done.[8]

Overall, centralized systems of authority, agenda-setting, human resource management, and accountability enhance the ability of public servants to provide non-partisan advice and service in support of fulfilling the cabinet's agenda. We have explained that these systems do not insulate the public service from the political realm. Indeed, the importance of being politically attuned has never been greater, given that the daily and hourly pressures of the political world have a direct impact on the priorities that define the government's agenda. Thus, bureaucrats

....

7 *Employment Equity Act*, S.C. 1995, c. 44, https://laws-lois.justice.gc.ca/eng/acts/E-5.401/index.html.

8 Trinh, "Report Reveals Widespread Discrimination."

operate in a multifaceted world of politics and public administration, requiring a high degree of political acumen.

Chapter Takeaways

This chapter observes that navigating the public service requires an appreciation that public administration is political.

- The centralization of power in government is clear, as is the authority of the partisan politicians in cabinet. Agendas are set and policy directives are issued from the centre of each government, and within the centre of each ministry, limiting the ability of rank-and-file public servants to define broad concepts like the public good.
- Governments are prone to reorganize themselves from time to time. This ensures the appropriate leadership and resources are in place to achieve key government priorities.
- To frame options and recommendations appropriately, a public servant must understand the formal and informal power dynamics within their unit, department, and government.
- Public servants need to be attuned to the world outside their cubicle or office. This situational awareness is key to understanding current challenges and anticipating opportunities to advance your government's agenda.
- Public servants require soft skills to bring people onside with a proposed course of action. Professional development courses can improve their ability to achieve results through people.
- Public servants are expected to provide expert, professional service in meeting the direction set by government. This is why they are hired largely on merit, with provisions designed to ensure the public service broadly reflects the public they serve.
- It is natural for public servants to feel like movable cogs in an impersonal bureaucratic machine. This feeling should not be confused with dispensability. Public servants play a critical role in ensuring that elected governments fulfill the mandates granted to them by voters.

CHAPTER 5

ATTRIBUTES OF A PUBLIC SERVANT

When considering all orders and levels of government, the public service is, by far, Canada's largest employer. This is not surprising, as government plays a role in nearly every aspect of our lives. Government funds and administers the building and maintenance of roads, hiring and training of teachers, protection of civil rights, regulation of businesses, and care for the sick and the elderly – the list of visible and invisible touchpoints seems never-ending. The resulting scope of positions in the public service is extensive, as are the number of job openings, even during periods of fiscal constraint. This broadness can be attractive to aspiring, new, and seasoned public servants alike. For those with knowledge of the system, there are often opportunities to move among different roles.

Roles and Functions

Canada's public service is not a single organization with seamless labour mobility. Instead, employees face considerable barriers when attempting to transition between federal, provincial, territorial, and municipal governments. Few operate as a unified employer from a human resources standpoint. Experience at one level is not always recognized or appreciated at another; the same is true within individual governments. Governments are separated into different ministries, departments, and agencies. Some staff work on the front lines interacting directly with the public while others have desk jobs behind the scenes. Others work remotely on some days, and in the office other days. Others still work remotely all of the time. While most public servants are situated in capital cities, many live and work in other places. Indeed, of all Government of Canada employees, fewer than half live in the Ottawa capital region.[1]

There are many positions and classifications within each functional area, from entry-level to management. The positions situated closest to executive decision-making typically reside in policy and strategy. These range from research or analyst positions in line departments, such as health or education, to policy coordination in the central unit of a department or central agency, to serving as an executive advisor to a senior or executive manager.

The most numerous and publicly visible roles are in operations. These include front-line workers delivering programs and services directly to the public or stakeholders. Program administrators develop reports and distribute grants. Regulators and inspectors oversee program implementation. Technical/professional roles are less visible, and include legal and scientific advisors, medical services experts, and others. They also encompass hundreds of shared services personnel that deliver crucial functions across departments, including occupational health and safety, information management, communications, building management, fleet management, information-technology support, legal services, human resources, financial management, and the like. Arguably the most thankless work lies in the general services, trades, and administrative support areas. These public servants provide secretariat, maintenance, facilities, and other forms of support.

A typical department or agency features a full complement of roles. Indeed, no public service functions effectively without high-performing staff and solid leadership in all areas. This requires public servants to develop experience and expertise in particular fields. It used to be common for employees to spend their entire careers in policy or operations roles. They would move among different government departments and/or into leadership or management positions within their field. Today a focus on flow between roles and functions is emerging.

A public service can deliver on policy demands only if there is effective collaboration across these functional areas. Any office worker who has tried to complete time-sensitive research or correspondence without access to the Internet can appreciate the importance of IT professionals to a well-functioning public service. By the same token, strategies and policies must account for the corporate and operational resources required to deliver on them. Operations and technical/ professional work rely on an appreciation for the intent behind particular policies and strategies.

For these reasons, top public service leaders promote understanding and collaboration through teamwork. They mobilize groups of public servants with a variety of functional responsibilities and assign them a common task or project. Managers aim to provide professional development opportunities for staff who are willing to transition into new functional areas. Nevertheless, some of the public service's deepest occupational barriers continue to separate staff in these various fields, notwithstanding departmental silos.

Despite the emerging trend, it remains uncommon to see public servants move across these functional areas. Each field requires unique sets of skills and knowledge, and each often constitutes a separate, insular community with its own unique culture. Stereotypes persist that administrative professionals and technical professionals are not cut out for policy work. Hiring managers in operations might think that people with policy and strategy experience are too distant from the front lines to offer quality service. There are, no doubt, public servants who have worked their way from the boiler room or mailroom to the boardroom. However, such anecdotes can be misleading in terms of establishing a realistic career path within the public service.

An additional consideration is that some public service roles require specialized expertise, credentials, and experience. For instance, in practice, deputy attorneys general require legal training. Likewise, nurse consultants who deliver public health initiatives must have applicable credentials. Conversely, all sorts of occupations, ranging from professional engineer to traffic warden, need not have any university-level public administration or political science training to succeed in a government career.

Nonetheless, public services often take a government-wide approach to senior leadership development and mobility. Ministers and deputy ministers might have backgrounds that are indirectly related to their department. Most senior public servants are expected to take on various roles across multiple ministries to develop the skills, knowledge, and networks essential for advancing the government's agenda. Early career professionals may benefit by acquiring cross-ministry experience for the same reason.

Building Competencies

Regardless of your career stage, success as a government employee hinges on having the right combination of knowledge, skills, and personal attributes to effectively carry out your responsibilities. These assets are competencies. They form the basis of public sector recruitment, development, and succession planning in Canada. Governments across the country have remarkably similar competency models, which is reflected in the relative consistency of public service work across Canada. It is complemented by the fact that public service commissions tend to contract the same management consulting firms to help develop and refine models.

What skill sets and abilities are most valued in the public service? Competency models are publicly available for the federal government and most provinces. You can consult public service commission or human resources (HR) websites, or contact their HR professionals, to gain access to their respective models. In general, governments value multiple clusters of competencies among their public servants: the ability to build and maintain relationships among colleagues, clients, partners, and stakeholders; the capacity to achieve results through planning and commitment; strengths across different modes of thinking; leadership capabilities, which are often captured by the notion of political acumen, discussed in **Chapter 4**; effective communication using multiple channels to inform and persuade different audiences; a passion and capacity for self-development; and business-related abilities.

Governments place high value on soft skills. Before being hired or promoted, the ideal public servant will possess social and emotional intelligence and work well with others. Prospective employees are rarely recruited solely because of their education credentials and hard skills, and existing personnel cannot expect to move up to the management ranks based solely on subject matter expertise and seniority. Governments insist that public servants demonstrate integrity and ethics, listen actively to colleagues and clients, engage in teamwork, and exude collegiality and inclusiveness. These expectations are outlined in codes of employee behaviour and in learning and development catalogues. Public service is a collective endeavour, which is why almost all public servants must demonstrate the capacity to work effectively in many sorts of teams. These groups bring together different roles, responsibilities, perspectives, and skill sets. Teams may be formally established in organizational charts or through terms of reference. Just as often, they can be fluid and ad hoc, involving various individuals from different units at different times. Sometimes teams are highly productive. They can be effective forums to brainstorm, plan, implement, and evaluate a specific task; participants find synergy and deliver quality work on time. Other teams are filled with tension. A single abrasive personality disrupts an otherwise harmonious work environment; the team leader's role is unclear, or their expectations are onerous or nonexistent; meetings are too frequent or infrequent, and frustrating or unproductive; or perhaps the team needs management to express a clear will to proceed with a proposed course of action. Chances are that throughout your career you will encounter all these scenarios and more. You will need to build and apply your professional competencies to get the most out of these collaborative efforts.

In addition to collaboration skills, governments demand that public servants demonstrate initiative and autonomy in their respective roles. Employees must be agile, resilient, curious, and accountable. Governments often distinguish between employees' capacity to reason in analytical, critical, and systems thinking. This demands that public servants discern trends and patterns, identify process improvements, and position their work in the context of the broader government environment. Other desired competencies include awareness of innovation, long-term thinking, and institutional memory.[2]

Many public servants are called upon to communicate to various audiences. In **Chapter 3**, we provided tips on how best to craft memorandums to cabinet and briefing notes for senior public servants, for instance. Policy analysts are just as likely to be asked to draft responses to members of the public, whether by working with communications specialists to develop key messages or speaking notes for ministers or writing responses to public letters and emails. The latter situate public

....
2 Baskoy, Evans, and Shields, "Assessing Policy Capacity in Canada's Public Services."

servants as a link between the public and government and require special tact in communicating information, empathy, and the minister's position. Mastering a government's preferred writing style takes practice, as does knowing when to adapt or pivot from it.

Tip: Be Mindful of Bureaucratese
Public servants use words and expressions that can confuse non-specialists. They favour precision (e.g., "facilitate" instead of "help," "terminate" instead of "end") and obscure expressions (e.g., "holistic approach," "go-forward basis"). They capitalize to denote authority (e.g., the "Prime Minister") and they overuse acronyms. The public service develops its own style of speech, such as dropping the article when referring to central agencies – a report might refer to "the PCO," whereas amongst themselves public servants might say, "We need to submit this to PCO." This language might work well internally, but when engaging with the public, it is important to strike a balance between formality and an accessible communication style.

The formidable list of qualities that seasoned public servants possess can be daunting to new professionals looking to advance in their careers. Students and recent graduates seeking an entry-level position in government might worry that they lack appropriate skills, training, and experience. How do you go about measuring and developing your competencies in these areas?

You already possess many of these qualities. It is usually a matter of recognizing and tying them to specific experiences that you have encountered. One effective approach is to demonstrate your competencies by sharing stories that showcase how you have applied them in real situations. In a job interview, public sector employers will express limited interest in your schooling, in the professional development courses that you took, or even the positions you held. They are far more interested in the lessons you learned (knowledge), the talents you acquired (skills), and the reputation you developed (attributes) that can be applied to the position for which you have applied. This requires a high level of self-awareness and the ability to provide examples of your experiences.

To develop your competencies, it helps to discuss your performance with people with whom you worked most closely, be they supervisors/instructors, peers/colleagues, or people who you led in team/group situations. Simple questions such as "What is one time you have seen me communicate effectively?" or "What's the single best way for me to improve myself as a team player?" can go a long way toward assessing and improving your competencies. Formal versions of these 360-degree assessments are common development tools within public service organizations. Simple, but frank, discussions over coffee with a mentor or colleague can provide you with feedback to identify strengths, weaknesses, and ways forward. The further that you progress in your career, the more potential information you can glean from these conversations, which will help you build confidence and identify areas for personal and professional growth.

Networking is another important component for improving your performance and advancing your career. The adage "It's not what you know, but who you know" extends beyond managers willing to hire familiar candidates. Recall that the public service has rules in place to prevent such practices (**Chapter 4**). Building broad and deep networks of public and private sector colleagues, both in-person and online, holds several advantages. Networking demonstrates your capacity for relationship-building and enhances your ability to think systemically. A pre-existing network is seen as an asset and potential resource for prospective employers, particularly with respect to roles involving stakeholder and client engagement. A personal network can alert you to upcoming employment opportunities, allowing you to explore and prepare in advance. Colleagues can provide direct referrals for unadvertised positions. You can communicate with mentors to provide advice and honest competency assessments that enhance your development. Furthermore, a broad network can allow you to explore both different fields of work and your interests.

Forging Your Career Path

Full-time, permanent public servants are shielded from the worst elements of the precarious work economy. Compared with workers in other sectors, they enjoy greater job and income security, competitive wages, pension plans, insurance benefits, including medical and dental coverage, and vacation time. Work-life balance is often better, with regular hours, rather than shiftwork, being a feature of public service roles, although work can drift into personal time, as with any job. The public service can be more amenable to remote work as well as paid sick days and leave for family-related responsibilities. For those starting out, there are student employment programs and even tuition rebates; for those who climb the ranks, there is generous executive pay and benefits. Government recruiters add that key selling points include the ability to make a difference and to find a career that matches employees' passion and commitment to diversity. These rewards come with the public service bargain we outlined in **Chapters 1** and **2**.

Most public servants turn to federal or provincial job boards when they are looking for a new position within the public service. This is where they will find publicly available postings in a variety of different departments. Some government job posting websites allow users to filter listings by job type (e.g., policy, operations, service, technical) or location, allowing you to narrow your search to cities and towns in which you are interested in living. Increasingly, jobs are listed as on-site, remote, or hybrid, giving an indication of the extent to which you can work from home. In addition to qualifications, specific criteria may include security level and language requirement. These job board advertisements are only the tip of the iceberg when it comes to available positions in the public service.

> **Tip: Keep Your Career Options Open**
> Sign up for job alerts from a variety of government job boards and online services. Internal opportunities and positions with other governments that you've never considered may arise. Don't wait until you feel the urge to move to a new position.

Many open positions are not publicly advertised because they are restricted to internal applicants, usually permanent employees within the organization (see **Chapter 4**). This may be due to a desire to hire people with specific experience within the government or department, or it could be because of collective bargaining rules that require union members to have the first opportunity to apply. In times of fiscal restraint, many governments will apply rules restricting the number of positions that can be posted publicly. These external hiring freezes help keep down costs by limiting the number of new employees. They also create internal competition for talent and often set off chain reactions of hiring as people move to new positions and leave old roles vacant. Sometimes managers are forced to declare failed searches when internal applicants fail to meet their standards. In those instances, they may apply for permission to post the position to the public. Job seekers who establish contact with employees inside government can anticipate these sorts of opportunities by asking about postings on internal job boards. The opportunity to apply for an exclusive category of internal positions is a further advantage of working in the public service.

Governments often offer a range of paid work-integrated learning programs, such as practicums, internships, or co-operative education opportunities, that are advertised outside the formal job boards. These limited-term positions allow current university students and recent graduates to gain entry-level experience in a particular sector, department, or field. Unique programs exist for people from equity-deserving groups, including Indigenous Peoples and people with disabilities, while others require special graduate-level training in business, economics, or public policy. Many governments have realized that they are competing for top talent and have created attractive opportunities that include competitive compensation packages and guaranteed permanent employment or streamlined processes for future hiring. For certain positions, employers must weigh applicants' interest in working from home against the benefits of in-person collaboration with coworkers. In addition to gaining work experience, building networks, and forging relationships with potential mentors, student employees can try out a career path or area of specialization to help them decide whether it is right for them. As well, they may be eligible to be "bridged in," a mechanism that allows them to be hired without being subject to the lengthy government hiring process.

As a co-operative education placement or internship concludes, a student might want to talk with their supervisor to identify a job title that represents the placement experience, if one was not assigned. They could write out a job description, if one did not exist. They ought to send a thank-you letter/card to the workplace supervisor and create a list of contacts from the work placement. As well, they should add content to a career portfolio, including a letter of reference, performance evaluation, brochures, written work, printouts of online contributions, and any other applicable materials to document what work was involved. This might require obtaining approvals from the employer, as appropriate. Many public service positions exist outside government departments. Government job boards are maintained by public service commissions who coordinate human resources for all units that fall within non-partisan central agencies and line departments, such as health, education, defence, or environment. They are not responsible for hiring or promoting public servants in agencies, boards, or commissions, however. For the numerous policy positions available in Indigenous governments, health authorities, municipal governments, school boards, universities, regulatory agencies, and more, job seekers should consult organization-specific job boards. Public service commissions do not handle job postings for political staff, which are typically unadvertised and rely on networking in partisan circles.

The formalities of a government job hiring process (see Box 4.1) raise important considerations for what to include in your job application materials. The most important objective in a cover letter and résumé is to convince the audience that you are the right person for that specific position. Many job seekers miss the mark by failing to tailor their application to the needs of the employer. Keep in mind that the application process is not foremost about you as a candidate; it is about the team you are looking to join, and you need to establish what you would contribute to their success. The formalities of the merit system make it essential to tailor your application to the specific job advertisement. Submitting a generic application significantly increases the likelihood of being deemed unsuitable, especially in contrast to applications that emphasize key details from the ad and clearly illustrate how the candidate's experience aligns with the requirements.

Preparing a strong application requires thoroughly reviewing both the job advertisement and the more detailed job description. The latter may be included with the ad, but not always. Asking HR personnel for a copy of the fuller job description will provide greater insights into the role, allowing you to refine your application as well as assess whether it is a position that truly appeals to you. The job description may be daunting. Here, it is important to keep in mind that very few applicants possess all of the qualities listed. Many are considered assets or areas of growth, meaning that a manager may be inclined to hire someone who has room to develop in the role. In fact, many managers prefer that route as it allows them to cultivate a longer-term relationship with the employee, improving retention and helping them to realize the benefits of their investment of time and resources into their training. In other words, consider applying even if you do not meet all the qualifications for the position as advertised. On occasion, a hiring manager might spot something in your background that serves as an equivalency. Expressing an interest to develop the sorts of skills and experience stated in the job ad can be attractive to certain managers. It may also help you gain an interview if no one else meets the advertised requirements.

When pursuing a position in public administration, it is useful to understand the organization's hiring process. For most governments, job postings are crafted and screened by HR professionals in consultation with the manager who will be overseeing the new employee. They help to ensure that the process follows the merit principle, including avoiding hiring biases. For all their strengths and professionalism, most HR professionals have little day-to-day contact with the people they help hire. They are skilled in process and can provide managers with guidance, however they seldom have detailed knowledge about the posted job itself. Many HR staff serve dozens of hiring managers each month, working on several job searches at once. In this environment, they rely heavily on the job advertisement to determine who to screen into a shortlist of potential candidates.

While processes differ from organization to organization, many large-scale searches involve a triaging process. HR professionals examine dozens (if not hundreds) of applications by verifying whether applicants meet the minimum requirements for the position, and whether they possess the required skills, knowledge, and competencies. This often involves using a check-list approach, quickly skimming each application to determine whether these criteria are met. Knowing this, successful job seekers ensure they explicitly mention their qualifications in their cover letters and résumés. If a job advertisement states that a certain post-secondary degree is required, they list it in their résumé. If a specific number of years of related experience is required, they list the months they worked in each full-time position along with a brief description of how the role aligns with the one being advertised. If the job posting has a list of key competencies, they incorporate the exact terminology in their cover letter. Making it easy on HR to verify you meet the requirements is key to being screened in and deemed eligible for the next phase of identifying who to invite for an interview and/or test. Many hiring managers trust their HR partners to create a long list of a dozen or so top candidates for the position. Unless you get past the HR screener, the manager may never see your résumé or cover letter. Once it lands on the manager's desk, they take a closer look at each applicant's professional background and communication skills to determine whether there appears to be a fit with the type of person they are looking to hire. Often, this involves examining intangible qualities that are not mentioned in the formal job description. You might have relevant lived, volunteer, or academic experience that pertains to the advertised position. This is where customizing each job application becomes essential, which is why it is advisable to avoid listing unrelated qualities. While experience working as a barista at a coffee shop may be relevant for someone applying for a junior position with consumer protection or economic development, for example, it could undermine a job application for a position in intergovernmental relations.

For job seekers who have worked with a political party, it is essential to exercise political acumen by being strategic in how this experience is presented on a résumé. Working as a politician's constituency assistant or volunteering on election campaigns can be framed as imparting valuable skills in correspondence-writing and public relations. Similarly, roles in ministerial offices enhance the political acuity that many senior managers are seeking. Highlighting these specific skills and competencies on a résumé is worthwhile. Less important is listing the specific politician or political party you served. In fact, name-dropping and disclosure of party affiliation may be detrimental to your application if the hiring manager disagrees with your political views or, more commonly, if they view your choice to include it as a poor reflection on your political judgment and ability to be non-partisan. This caution is recommended regardless of which political party is in power.

Even though privacy rules and human rights protections may raise ethical and legal questions about an employer consulting a job applicant's social media, some government HR professionals and hiring managers will nevertheless look at a prospective employee's online presence to identify red flags and positive endorsements. Hiring managers may also turn to a candidate's online profiles to inform their decision, irrespective of privacy considerations. What they find can boost, hinder, or even disqualify an applicant's perceived suitability for a role.

Engagement in online communities is an increasingly essential practice for today's public servants. Many governments have social media tools for the use of their employees. Likewise, many communities of practice and professional organizations offer online forums to connect their members. The wider world of social media is another networking tool that is a great source for career intelligence and professional development tips. Using a profile with your own name does not obligate you to post online content. Many public servants do not, preferring to simply observe online discussions and follow opinion leaders in their field. Anonymous social media profiles may allow you to join conversations without revealing your identity, although you can expect your voice to carry less weight.

Tips on developing a solid and positive digital profile abound online. For example, the featured skills and endorsements section of a LinkedIn profile should emphasize the core competencies expected of public servants (see earlier sections in this chapter). Members of your network should be able to vouch for your talents in those areas. Above all, be cognizant of what you post. A positive online reputation is of growing importance if you want to achieve your career goals.

Many public servants are rightly cautious about using social media for professional purposes. They worry about contravening codes of behaviour or government policies if they publicly communicate about political and policy issues. These trepidations have merit. To avoid trouble, public servants should not comment on matters that concern their area of work, and they should be wary about identifying themselves as government employees on their social media platforms. Where social media debates and public servants are concerned, when in doubt, it is usually best not to engage. Job candidates must be equally careful.

Tip: Manage Your Digital Footprint

Assume that current and future employers will have access to anything online about you. Even conversations that you assume to be private can have implications for your career. The sagest advice may be to ask yourself the following: Would I be comfortable if my direct supervisor found out about this post? Would I want someone to repost this years later to cause embarrassment or stir trouble? If the answer is maybe, it's best to consult. If it's no, and you value your job, it's best to sit it out.

If you are fortunate enough to land a government job interview, it is likely to be heavily structured and scripted, with a hiring committee or board taking turns reading carefully designed questions word-for-word. In these scenarios, all candidates are treated in a reasonably identical fashion to contribute to an objective hiring decision. The interviewers might have gone through interview training and, wherever possible, the same group of interviewers will participate in all interviews. The interview is often formal and impersonal, and the questions focus on the job and its requirements. The interviewers will dutifully take notes throughout and might use a scoring system. One or more tests might be administered, such as a briefing note assignment. Conversely, in some cases a job interview may entail an unstructured conversation with spontaneous questions and limited notetaking.

Table 5.1 contains a list of questions you might encounter depending on the nature of the job. If you have difficulty answering, you may need to develop competency in that area. Note that official-language proficiency might be evaluated for a position with some governments, particularly the Government of Canada.

Evidently, interviewers are interested in assessing far more than a candidate's educational or work experience qualifications. The interview is likely to probe responses to hypothetical scenarios so that interviewers can consider how the candidate would handle a situation relevant to the job. A candidate may also be asked to describe a relevant experience that allows the interviewer to consider their behaviour, as well as specific educational and professional knowledge relevant to the job, which enables them to test the veracity of the information they are sharing.[3] There can

....
3 Public Service Commission of Canada, *Structured Interviewing*.

TABLE 5.1 Potential Questions in a Public Sector Job Interview

COMPETENCY	KNOWLEDGE QUESTIONS	SKILLS QUESTIONS	ATTRIBUTES QUESTIONS
Achievement	What did you learn from your last big success? Your last failure?	How have you learned to produce results under stress?	What would your supervisors say about your ability to deliver results?
Business	How do you go about drafting a budget?	When have you had to accomplish more with less, and how did you do it?	What illustrates your commitment to fiscal responsibility?
Communication	What are the biggest barriers to people understanding you?	What's the most you've ever written in the shortest amount of time, and what helped you most?	When did you clearly convey a difficult message, and how did the audience respond?
Leadership	Which leadership model aligns best with your approach?	How have you generated consensus among disparate interests?	What would your followers say about you?
Relationships	Which course, book, or film taught you most about human interaction?	How do you resolve conflict with your supervisors?	What would your peers say about you?
Self-Development	What's the one area you hope to develop through your next work experience?	How do you ensure you learn from your mistakes?	What's the best demonstration of your commitment to lifelong learning?
Thinking	What's your go-to model for problem-solving?	When was the last time you thought quickly on your feet?	How do you ensure your work makes a positive impact on the broader system?

also be job simulations whereby a candidate is asked to show that they can carry out relevant work, such as if they are given information and asked to analyze it on the spot.

Afterwards, members of the hiring committee compare the responses and assess the candidates' suitability against the job description and overall fit. Reference checks typically follow once a consensus is reached on ranking the candidates. Advertising the job, screening applicants for suitability, holding a structured interview process, administering testing, and a committee deliberating whether to offer a job to a candidate are key features of the merit principle to hire the best possible candidate in a fair and equitable manner. Thorough documentation of all stages of the job hiring process is another feature, in case a decision is challenged.

Finding Fit in the Public Service

As with any organization, starting a new job or role in government can be disorienting at first as you become acquainted with new colleagues, new responsibilities, and potentially new surroundings. Onboarding in government can place much of the onus on the employee to figure out which coworkers have institutional memory, who has policy knowledge, who gets things done quickly, and who is well-connected. Reading your collective agreement provides additional information about the role, including benefits and entitlements. New employees should monitor their paycheques to ensure that all is in order and, if applicable, investigate the portability of a previous workplace pension.

Working for the first time in government can be a culture shock. For some people, the size of the workforce, the variety of supports, the job stability, and the vastness of public resources take getting used to. The opportunity to make a difference to society can also be new. For others, the shock of working in a maze of cubicles, the glacial speed of moving files forward, and the impersonality of working in a government setting can be a surprise. With time, energetic and idealistic employees with ideas for change will become familiar with the fact that government has a process-driven organizational culture. Public policy reform is usually slow, measured, and careful. It involves researching options along with considerable internal consultation, as well as stakeholder input and a scan of the public appetite for change. Most importantly, the political will must exist or else a proposal will fall flat (as discussed in **Chapter 3**).

For those who secure a public service position, the focus often turns to finding the right fit within the organization. Research illustrates that employees tend to choose jobs that allow them to be genuine at work, maintain healthy lives away from the job, and achieve a positive sense of achievement.[4] When these three components – authenticity, balance, and challenge – are out of sync, people tend to search for other opportunities. In many ways, public service jobs are like other workplaces: some folks have a difficult time finding fit within their team's culture, finding their feet at work and at home, and finding the right level of engagement. There are some unique features of public service work that set it apart, however.[5]

On occasion, public servants may experience dissonance between their own values and those of the government they serve. This tension is acute for people tasked with implementing policy changes that fly in the face of personal conviction or the evidence they have presented through briefings. Discussed at length throughout this book, the public servant's duty is to provide that sort of fearless advice and, even when it is not heeded, to loyally implement government directives provided they are legally sound. This is a key element of the public service bargain, and it prevents unelected bureaucrats from substituting their own vision of the public good for that of democratically elected officials. Acting on a decision that you disagree with may be easier said than done, especially on matters of conscience or when there are likely to be negative implications for people's lives or livelihoods. As mentioned, if a public servant cannot abide by such direction, they ought to ask for reassignment, search out new positions, or seek whistleblower protection. Leaking information or otherwise acting insubordinately could result in disciplinary action, dismissal, or even criminal prosecution.

For some public servants, it can be difficult to find the time and energy to meet both professional and personal goals. They must cope with the demands of an increasingly complex and expansive public sector, governments bent on achieving change within four-year election cycles and constricting budgets, and 24-7 news cycles and electronic communication. These pressures cascade, placing stress on employees further down the hierarchy. One response is workplace flexibility, which allows them to adapt their schedules or work from home, if they

....

4 Banks, McCauley, Gardner, and Guler, "A Meta-analytic Review."
5 Johnston, "New Development."

meet certain performance targets. These part-time, flextime, flex-place solutions appear to meet the demands of today's workers. Remote work is becoming more common in a competitive job market and is being raised in collective bargaining negotiations.

Flexwork allows employees to shift their workday hours so that they can schedule their work around their personal circumstances. Employees are better able to attend to personal responsibilities, such as childcare obligations and caring for aging family members, managing health issues and medical appointments, and participating in seasonal hunting and agriculture activities.[6] Hybrid or fully remote work offers additional flexibility, allowing employees to save time and money by not having to commute to the office. People with disabilities can benefit from the reduced barriers that working from home offers. Interest is growing as a response to broader policy objectives, such as traffic congestion and climate change, and as video conferencing becomes a preferred way to hold meetings.

There are some downsides to remote work and flexible hours. Negative public optics, instances of misuse, and the potential for inequality among different roles – particularly with jobs that must be carried out in-person, such as first responders, transportation workers, and custodial staff – are significant barriers to implementing workplace flexibility policies. Team culture can suffer when remote workers do not personally interact. Some politicians voice concern about inequities versus the private sector and how remote work contributes to the hollowing out of downtowns, which makes local businesses vulnerable and weakens public transit ridership. Generous benefits enjoyed by public servants draw the ire of critics, which keeps politicians and senior public servants mindful of extending them too far. For their part, many public sector and union leaders view themselves as setting workplace standards that ought to encourage similar practices elsewhere. The extent to which public servants benefit from these considerations differs from place to place and time to time, and whether flexwork and remote work improves or weakens productivity and job satisfaction is often circumstantial.

....

6 Champagne, Choinière, and Granja, "Government of Canada's Teleworking and Hybrid Policies."

Professional Development

There are many opportunities available for public servants who are interested in professional development. Secondments, temporary stretch assignments, and cross-department working groups can build the competencies of an early career public servant seeking to expand their networks, knowledge, and skill sets. Formal interchanges with other organizations and task team assignments can do the same for seasoned public servants.

Governments often support employees who are keen to build knowledge and skill sets, ranging from second-language training to updating their technical skills. Executive leadership programs exist for professionals seeking to move up the management ranks. Some public sector employers will consider supporting an employee who requests time off and financial support to enroll in a course or program offered by a post-secondary institution or professional association. The Canada School of Public Service offers a suite of courses, programs, and events for federal public servants. Another way to develop competencies and find fit is through professional development books and online resources.

To round out your development, a public servant should seek out hands-on learning opportunities. These forms of relational and experiential learning are most likely to generate the stories and references necessary to succeed in job applications and interviews. Coaching and mentorship programs can link experienced hands with those who have less public sector experience. Coaches typically offer short-term skills development and career counselling support for a fee. Mentors provide longer-term, more holistic support for professional growth at no cost. Finding the right coach or mentor is a process that involves a combination of referrals and online searches. Being part of a recognized program or having positive references from respected colleagues will go a long way to ensuring a successful relational learning experience.

Beyond this, people may seek out volunteer opportunities with non-profit organizations whose work resembles or interacts with the public sector. Serving on a board of directors or volunteering for working committees can provide critical experience with strategy development, project planning, budget management, communications, and teamwork. Such extracurricular activity builds a professional network.

Table 5.2 outlines developmental ideas in competency areas, including formal, relational, and experiential opportunities. By being

TABLE 5.2 Learning Opportunities for a Career in the Public Service

COMPETENCY CLUSTER	IN SCHOOL	IN A VOLUNTARY ORGANIZATION	IN GOVERNMENT
Achievement	Lead at least one extracurricular project to completion	Assist in the organization's strategic planning	Invite a known innovator to be your mentor
Business	Review literature on public finance	Shadow a treasurer	Debrief with a financial officer after budget season
Communication	Take/teach effective writing clinics	Assist with a voluntary organization's social media strategy	Ask to observe verbal briefings with senior personnel or solicit feedback on your briefings
Leadership	Serve on a student club board	Offer to mentor new members of the voluntary organization	Teach a development course in your area of expertise
Relationships	Select classes with group work	Organize networking events	Take social intelligence training
Self-Development	Participate in professional development workshops	Take on new tasks outside your comfort zone to develop resilience	Engage in 360-degree competency assessments
Thinking	Take courses or workshops in systemic design	Identify challenges in common with other voluntary organizations and partner to solve them	Attend/organize cross-government events to develop organizational awareness

purposeful and creating learning opportunities like these, public servants can build a broad repertoire of knowledge, skills, and experiences to support job applications, interviews, and performance reviews. In your own career, you may benefit from documenting the personal attributes you employ or acquire whenever you overcome a challenging situation. A competency journal will be a useful resource as you prepare for the next stage in your career. Identifying your organization's key competencies is a great first step. Next, consider recording any instances in which you have the chance to demonstrate those abilities in your work. A running list in your notebook or notes app becomes a great resource any time you have a performance review or apply for a new position.

This chapter reinforces the main objective of this book: to inspire deeper learning about how government works in Canada and to equip readers with the tools to forge a meaningful career path in the public sector. We believe that being a public servant is much more than a job. It is a noble venture – one made even more rewarding if your professional purpose revolves around concepts like working with others to give back to your community, and more manageable if your focus centres on providing fearless advice and loyal implementation in service of the public good. *The Public Servant's Guide to Government in Canada* is just that: a set of suggestions for how to get the most out of your time in government.

Chapter Takeaways

This chapter explains that the varied roles and competencies of a public servant can be both exciting and daunting for early career professionals.

- A wide range of roles exists in the public service. Those with the right competencies, networks, and persistence can navigate a career that spans different sectors, fields, and governments.
- As the challenges facing governments cut across the same sorts of boundaries, public service leaders expect more from their employees in terms of their ability to communicate and collaborate with colleagues inside and outside government.
- Public servants need self-awareness and a commitment to self-development to build their careers.
- Relational and experiential learning (i.e., working with others in real-world environments) are generally more effective forms of learning than sitting in a classroom or reading.

GLOSSARY OF TERMS

accountability: A line of obligation that establishes which individuals and institutions are responsible for decisions.

agencies, boards, and commissions (ABCs): Government organizations that operate at arm's length from the government and ministers, such as Crown corporations.

agenda-setting: Competitive political activities that seek to put policy problems and solutions at the top of a government's list of priorities.

briefing note: A short, written summary that succinctly and objectively informs the reader about an issue.

cabinet: The prime minister (or premier) and ministers who are granted the constitutional authority to make government decisions on behalf of the Crown.

caretaker mode: The period surrounding a general election when the public service operates in a limited capacity, providing essential programs and services and refraining from advancing major policy decisions.

centre of government: The nucleus of decision-making among senior government personnel. In the Government of Canada, the centre is generally understood to include the Prime Minister's Office, the Privy Council Office, the Department of Finance, and the Treasury Board Secretariat.

clerk: The chief deputy minister and highest-ranking public servant. In the Government of Canada, this person heads up the Privy Council Office in Ottawa and serves as Secretary to Cabinet.

Crown: The institution representing the authority of the state in Canada, embodied by the reigning King, and exercised by the governor general and lieutenant governors.

democracy: The use of a free and fair election process for citizens to elect representatives who will represent their interests and oversee government.

deputy minister (DM): A public servant who is the senior leader of a government department and who serves at the pleasure of the government of the day.

federalism: A system of government whereby powers and responsibilities are constitutionally assigned to different orders of government, which cannot abrogate each other's areas of jurisdiction.

first minister: The prime minister or premier.

First Nations: Indigenous groups descendant from the earliest inhabitants of North America, other than Métis and Inuit.

governor general: The primary representative of the King or Queen of Canada. Exercises constitutional authorities such as appointing a federal cabinet, signing federal bills into law, and authorizing a federal election.

Indigenous Peoples: Members of First Nations, Métis, and Inuit communities.

Inuit: Indigenous Peoples with historic ties to the northern most lands in North America.

lieutenant governor: A representative of the King or Queen of Canada in each province. The lieutenant governor is appointed by the governor general on advice of the prime minister and federal cabinet, and likewise appoints a provincial cabinet, signs provincial bills into law, and authorizes a provincial election. In the territories, similar roles are fulfilled by commissioners.

majority government: The situation in which the governing party controls at least half of the seats in the legislature. In this case, bills will all but assuredly be passed.

memorandum to cabinet: A succinct analysis of a policy issue prepared by public servants that recommends a course of action to the executive branch. Also known as an MC or a cabinet report.

merit principle: The standard that public servants must be hired or promoted through an advertised formal job competition and on the basis of their competencies.

Métis: Indigenous Peoples of historic mixed First Nations and European ancestry who are accepted by a Métis community.

minister: A politician who is appointed to cabinet and is responsible for overseeing a department and/or a government agency or other portfolio.

minority government: The situation in which members of opposition parties collectively outnumber those of the governing party in the legislature. Since bills are subject to defeat, there is an onus on the governing party to consider the views of members of other parties.

New Political Governance (NPG): A theory that government is becoming politicized.

New Public Management (NPM): A theory that government is adopting businesslike management principles.

non-partisan: A perspective of political neutrality and objectivity that does not favour or align with any specific political party.

parliamentary secretary: A parliamentarian who has designated responsibilities to assist a minister but is not a member of cabinet. Also known as an associate minister.

permanent campaigning: The exploitation of public resources for campaign-like use by those in positions of political power.

political acumen: The ability to work effectively by applying knowledge of the political, economic, and organizational context, deft social skills, and ethics to achieve government objectives.

political staff: Impermanent, partisan political appointees who serve at the pleasure of the minister in whose office they are employed. Those working in the Prime Minister's Office or the Premier's Office tend to have considerable clout, particularly the chief of staff.

premier: The head of a provincial or territorial cabinet and typically the leader of the political party that controls the legislature.

Premier's Office: The central office in a provincial government that houses the premier and senior political staff.

prime minister: The head of the federal cabinet and the leader of the political party that controls the House of Commons.

Prime Minister's Office (PMO): The central office in the Government of Canada that houses the prime minister's most senior political advisors, such as the chief of staff, principal secretary, and director of communications, among others.

principal-agent problem: The concept that policy is not implemented the way that a decision-maker (the principal) originally envisioned because so many public servants and political staff (the agents) are involved in its development and implementation.

Privy Council Office (PCO): The central agency in Ottawa that consists of public servants, including the clerk, and operates as the bureaucratic, non-partisan counterpart to the Prime Minister's Office.

The provincial-level equivalent is often known as Executive Council Office or Cabinet Office.

public administration: The machinery of government that designs, delivers, and monitors public policies, programs, and services.

public policy: Government decisions and non-decisions that address public problems through rules and the allocation of resources.

public servants: Permanent employees of government, most of whom are hired based on the merit principle and possess specialized expertise. Otherwise known as bureaucrats and civil servants.

public service bargain: The implicit agreement between elected officials and public servants, defining their roles, responsibilities, and mutual expectations. It balances political leadership with professional, non-partisan advice and administration.

responsible government: A parliamentary system in which cabinet is accountable to the legislature.

Truth and Reconciliation Commission of Canada: A federal government commission that investigated the harms on Indigenous Peoples incurred by the Indian residential school system. In 2015, it issued ninety-four calls to action for repairing the relationship between Indigenous and non-Indigenous Peoples in Canada.

Weberian bureaucracy: The principle that a public service must feature an organizational hierarchy, specialized labour, impersonal processes, standardized employment practices, and job security.

BIBLIOGRAPHY

Althaus, Catherine, and Thea Vakil. "Political Transitions: Opportunities to
Renegotiate the Public Service Bargain." *Canadian Public Administration* 56,
no. 3 (September 2013): 478–90. https://doi.org/10.1111/capa.12031.

Aucoin, Peter. *The New Public Management: Canada in Comparative Perspective.*
Montreal: Institute for Research on Public Policy, 1995.

———. "New Political Governance in Westminster Systems: Impartial Public
Administration and Management Performance at Risk." *Governance: An
International Journal of Policy, Administration and Institutions* 25, no. 2 (April
2012): 177–99. https://doi.org/10.1111/j.1468-0491.2012.01569.x.

Auld, Graeme, Ashley Casovan, Amanda Clarke, and Benjamin Faveri.
"Governing AI through Ethical Standards: Learning from the Experiences
of Other Private Governance Initiatives." *Journal of European Public Policy* 29,
no. 11 (2012): 1822–44. https://doi.org/10.1080/13501763.2022.2099449.

Banks, George C., Kelly Davis McCauley, William L. Gardner, and Courtney
E. Gule. "A Meta-analytic Review of Authentic and Transformational
Leadership: A Test for Redundancy." *The Leadership Quarterly* 27, no. 4
(August 2016): 634–52. https://doi.org/10.1016/j.leaqua.2016.02.006.

Baskoy, Tuna, Bryan Evans, and John Shields. "Assessing Policy Capacity in
Canada's Public Services: Perspectives of Deputy and Assistant Deputy
Ministers." *Canadian Public Administration* 54, no. 2 (June 2011): 217–34.
https://doi.org/10.1111/j.1754-7121.2011.00171.x.

Birch, A.H. *Representative and Responsible Government: An Essay on the British
Constitution.* London: Routledge, 1964.

Brock, David M., and J.W.J. Bowden. "Beyond the Writ: The Expansion of
the Caretaker Convention in the Twenty-First Century." *Saskatchewan Law
Review* 87, no. 1 (2024): 1–50. https://canlii.ca/t/7nc90.

Champagne, Eric, Olivier Choinière, and Aracelly Denise Granja.
"Government of Canada's Teleworking and Hybrid Policies in the
Aftermath of the COVID-19 Pandemic." *Canadian Public Administration* 66,
no. 2 (June 2023): 158–75. https://doi.org/10.1111/capa.12520.

Cole, Rose. "Public Service Bargains and Non-partisan Ministerial Advisors: Servants of Two Masters." *International Review of Administrative Sciences* 88, no. 3 (September 2022): 757–73. https://doi.org/10.1177/0020852320955217.

Dye, Thomas. *Understanding Public Policy.* 3rd ed. Englewood Cliffs, NJ: Prentice-Hall, 1978.

Employment Equity Act, S.C. 1995, c. 44. https://laws-lois.justice.gc.ca/eng/acts/E-5.401/index.html.

Hall, Peter A. "Policy Paradigms, Social Learning, and the State: The Case of Economic Policymaking in Britain." *Comparative Politics* 25, no. 3 (April 1993): 275–96. https://doi.org/10.2307/422246.

Himelfarb, Alex. "The Intermestic Challenge." Speaking notes for an address to APEX Symposium, Ottawa, ON, June 5, 2002. https://epe.lac-bac.gc.ca/100/205/301/pco-bcp/website/07-08-14/www.pco-bcp.gc.ca/printer.asp@PrinterFriendly=1&Language=E&Page=Clerk&Sub=Clerks Speeches&Doc=20020605_apex_e.htm.

Honeghem, Annie, and Karolien Van Dorpe. "Performance Management Systems for Senior Civil Servants: How Strong Is the Managerial Public Service Bargain?" *International Review of Administrative Sciences* 79, no. 1 (March 2013): 9–27. https://doi.org/10.1177/0020852312467549.

Hood, Christopher, and Ruth Dixon. *A Government That Worked Better and Cost Less? Evaluating Three Decades of Reform and Change in UK Central Government.* Oxford: Oxford University Press, 2015. https://doi.org/10.1093/acprof:oso/9780199687022.001.0001.

Howlett, Michael, M. Ramesh, and Anthony Perl. *Studying Public Policy: Policy Cycles and Policy Subsystems.* 3rd ed. Don Mills, ON: Oxford University Press, 2009.

Jewell, Eva, and Ian Mosby. *Calls to Action Accountability: A 2023 Status Update on Reconciliation.* Toronto: Yellowhead Institute, 2023. https://yellowheadinstitute.org/trc/.

Johnston, Karen. "New Development: Is It Time for a New Public Service Bargain?" *Public Money & Management.* Published as Latest Articles, April 23, 2024. https://doi.org/10.1080/09540962.2024.2343168.

Kernaghan, Kenneth, and John Langford. *The Responsible Public Servant.* 2nd ed. Toronto: Institute of Public Administration of Canada, 2014.

Kingdon, John W. *Agendas, Alternatives, and Public Policies.* New York: Longman, 2011.

Macfarlane, Emmett. "The Place of Constitutional Conventions in the Constitutional Architecture, and in the Courts." *Canadian Journal of Political Science* 55, no. 2 (June 2022): 322–41. https://doi.org/10.1017/S0008423922000051.

Marland, Alex, Jared. J. Wesley, and Mireille Lalancette. *No "I" in Team: Party Loyalty in Canadian Politics.* Toronto: University of Toronto Press, 2025.

May, Kathryn. "Speaking Truth to Power Discouraged in Public Service." *Policy Options*, May 11, 2022. https://policyoptions.irpp.org/magazines /may-2022/report-public-service-fearful-advice.

Papillon, Martin. "Adapting Federalism: Indigenous Multilevel Governance in Canada and the United States." *Publius: The Journal of Federalism* 42, no. 2 (Spring 2012): 289–312. https://doi.org/10.1093/publius/pjr032.

Privy Council Office. "Guidance for Deputy Ministers." Government of Canada. Last modified December 13, 2017. https://www.canada.ca/en /privy-council/services/publications/guidance-deputy-ministers.html.

Public Service Commission of Canada. *Structured Interviewing: How to Design and Conduct Structured Interviews for an Appointment Process.* Ottawa: Public Service Commission of Canada, 2009. https://www.canada.ca/content /dam/canada/public-service-commission/migration/plcy-pltq/guides /structured-structuree/rpt-eng.pdf.

Savoie, Donald. *Breaking the Bargain: Public Servants, Ministers, and Parliament.* Toronto: University of Toronto Press, 2003. https://doi .org/10.3138/9781442657229.

Schaffer, Bernard. *The Administrative Factor.* London: Frank Cass, 1973.

Senate Canada. "How a Bill Becomes a Law." Accessed December 13, 2024. https://sencanada.ca/en/about/publications/how-a-bill-becomes-law/.

Sutherland, Sharon L., and G. Bruce Doern. *Bureaucracy in Canada: Control and Reform.* Toronto: University of Toronto Press, 1985.

Tait, John. "A Strong Foundation: Report of the Task Force on Public Service Values and Ethics (the Summary)." *Canadian Public Administration* 40, no. 1 (March 1997): 1–22. https://doi.org/10.1111/j.1754-7121.1997.tb01493.x.

Treasury Board Secretariat. "Population of the Federal Public Service by Province or Territory of Work." Government of Canada. Last modified July 11, 2024. https://www.canada.ca/en/treasury-board-secretariat /services/innovation/human-resources-statistics/population-federal -public-service-geographic-region.html.

Trinh, Judy. "Report Reveals Widespread Discrimination at Highest Level of Canada's Public Service." *CTV News*, July 30, 2024. https://www .ctvnews.ca/politics/report-reveals-widespread-discrimination-at -highest-level-of-canada-s-public-service-1.6981643.

Wardle, Claire, and Hossein Derakhshan. *Information Disorder: Toward an Interdisciplinary Framework for Research and Policymaking.* Vol. 27. Strasbourg: Council of Europe, 2017.

Wilson, Woodrow. "The Study of Administration." *Political Science Quarterly* 2, no. 2 (June 1887): 197–222. https://doi.org/10.2307/2139277.

INDEX

ABOUT THE AUTHORS

Alex Marland researches what goes on in the backrooms of Canadian politics. Along the way to becoming Jarislowsky Chair in Trust and Political Leadership at Acadia University in Nova Scotia, he was an analyst with Transport Canada in Ottawa and a director of communications with several departments in the Government of Newfoundland and Labrador. He has placed dozens of interns in public sector roles, has delivered multiple workshops to public servants about how government works, and routinely interviews politicians and political staff.

Jared J. Wesley is a pracademic – a practising political scientist and former public servant – whose career path to the University of Alberta's Department of Political Science has included senior management positions in the Alberta Public Service (APS). As Professor of Political Science, he studies and teaches the politics of bureaucracy and the bureaucracy of politics. He is also associate dean of graduate studies for the University of Alberta's Faculty of Arts and a member of the university's Black Faculty Collective.

Also by the authors: Alex Marland, Mireille Lalancette, and Jared J. Wesley, *No "I" in Team: Party Loyalty in Canada*, Toronto: University of Toronto Press, 2025, and Alex Marland and Jared J. Wesley, *Inside Canadian Politics*, 3rd edition, Oxford: Oxford University Press, 2025.